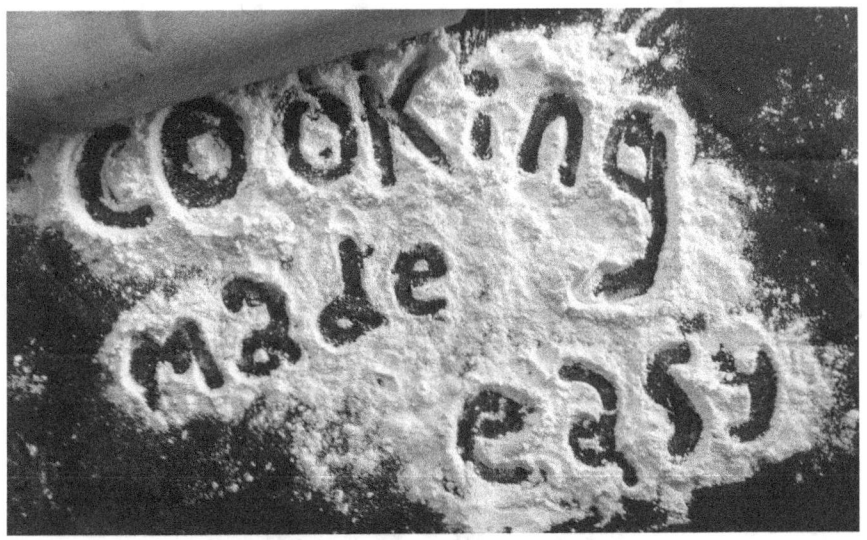

Air fryers work by circulating super-hot air, which quickly and evenly reaches all the surfaces of the food.
In other words, it gives food that crispy-fried texture and golden-brown color without having to actually deep-fry anything.

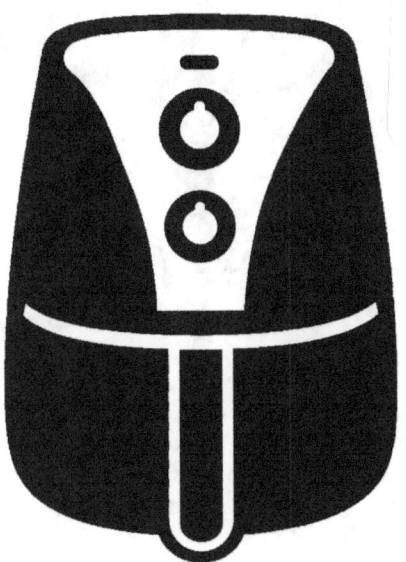

I0510246

By William Cato Jenkins Jr.

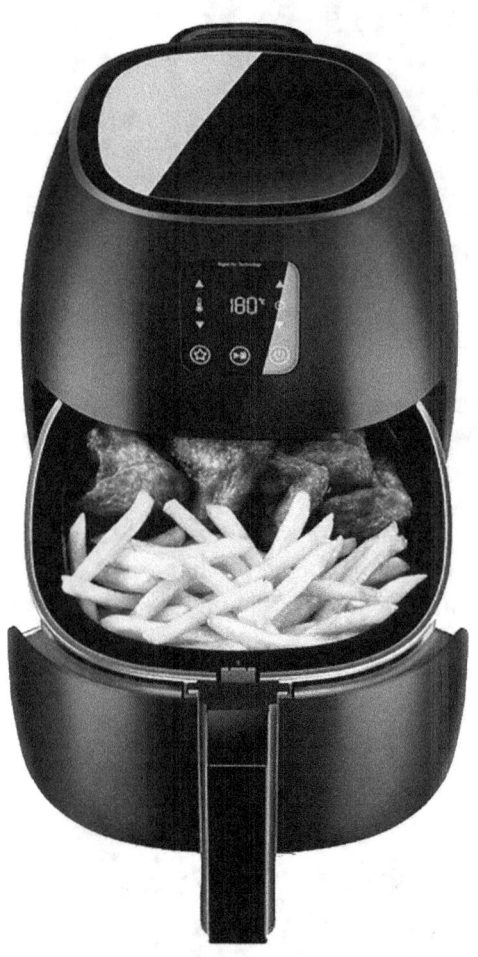

To Help you save more time in the kitchen, this book also features food preparation shortcuts, suggested timesaving substitutions, and clues on planning a head - all tried-and -proven ways of making meal preparation a fast and fun event in your household.

In a hurry? Don't fret! Just turn to this book Cooking Made Easy. You'll soon wonder how you ever managed without it.

2 COOKING MADE EASY...

Healthy fried food that's just as delicious as the real thing?

This isn't the stuff of legend. The air fryer is officially the go-to kitchen appliance of keto-dieters, Whole30 doers, and really anyone who is looking to enjoy healthier versions of crispy fries and chicken wings.

The gadget, which "fries" food using a small amount of oil and hot air to dehydrate and cook to get a crispy texture, has boomed in popularity within the last few years—and it doesn't appear to be dying down anytime soon. (Admit it: You totally had an air fryer on your holiday wish list.)

But is the hype really warranted? Does an air fryer actually make healthy eating easier? The experts have some thoughts.

Is air-fried food healthy?

Air-frying is definitely healthier than a regular fryer, says Rizzo. By slashing the oil, you're cutting a ton of calories and fat. The exact amount is hard to pinpoint, because cooking preparations can vary by machine and by person, but you're using a tablespoon of oil versus the whole quart used in traditional deep-frying, says Rizzo.

Plus, you can make a lot of veggie-heavy recipes taste just as satisfying as an order of fries, says White. "Some of my favorites are quinoa stuff peppers, sweet potato hash, asparagus wrapped with crispy prosciutto, and zucchini ribbons with fresh herbs," she says. Yum!

What are the best ways to use an air-fryer?

Of course, the air fryer is a great option for lighter chicken wings and French fries but it's also ideal for making healthier versions of breaded fish, pizza, and even cakes, says White. "For best results, I suggest always preheating the machine before cooking and be sure to clean the machine well between each use. Crumbs can accumulate in the bottom of the unit, which can burn and smoke," she says.

You don't always need a recipe. "I usually use my air fryer for from-scratch cooking, but I'll occasionally put some easy convenience foods like bagged frozen sweet potato fries in the air fryer," says White. "They come out so much better than baking them in the oven on a sheet pan."

Air fryers are small ovens
with a highly concentrated
heat source and powerful fan
that moves the hot air around
to crisp up wings, fries,
veggies and more
air-fried recipes with little (or
zero!) oil. They create a nice
"fried" finish that your oven
range can't compete with, as
well as, reheating results that
blow away the
average microwave.
Plus, an air fryer requires only
a small amount of oil to make
foods crispy with a fraction
of the calories and fat of
traditional cooking methods,
like deep frying.

Contents

Vegetables 8

Seafood 20

Poulty&Meat 30

Desserts 42

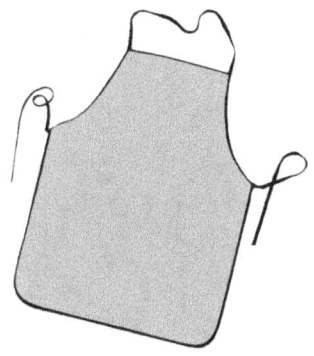

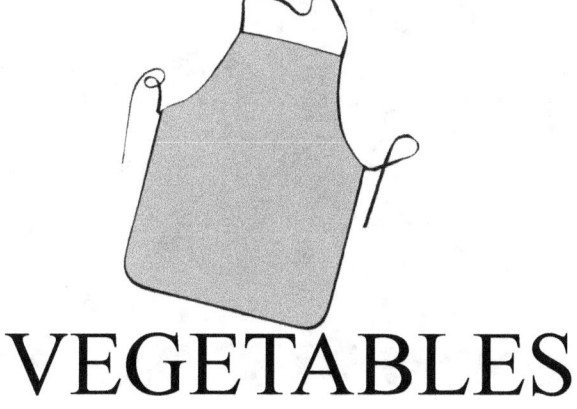

VEGETABLES

Crispy Air-Fryer Baked Potatoes

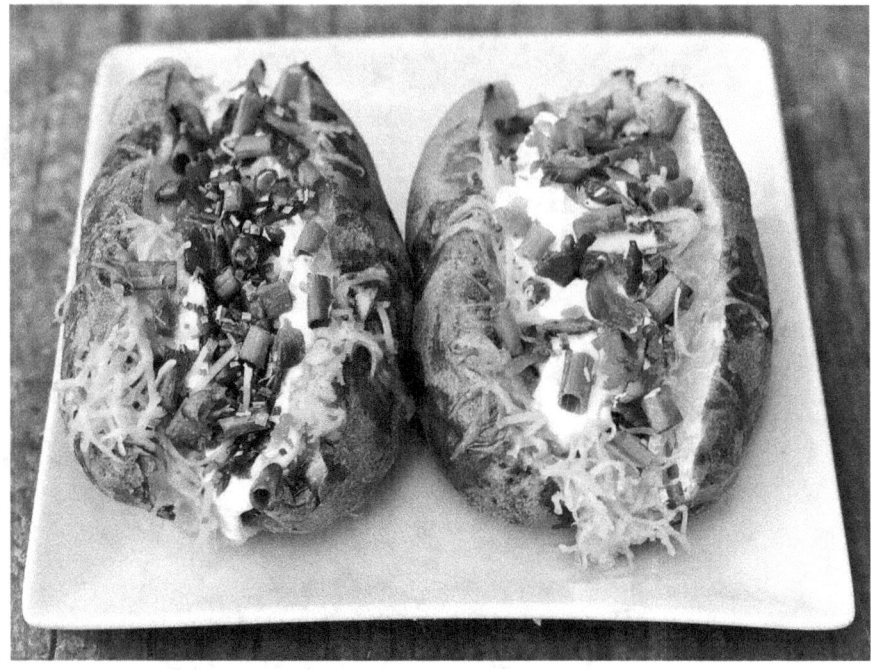

Ingredients

- 2 Large Russet Potatoes, Scrubbed
- 1 Tablespoon Peanut Oil
- ½ Teaspoon Coarse Sea Salt

prep: 5 mins
cook: 1 hr
total: 1 hr 5 mins
Servings: 2
Yield: 2 baked potatoes

Directions

Step 1 - Preheat air fryer to 400 degrees F (200 degrees C).

Step 2 - Brush potatoes with peanut oil and sprinkle with salt. Place them in the air fryer basket and place basket in the air fryer.

Step 3 - Cook potatoes until done, about 1 hour. Test for doneness by piercing them with a fork.

Air-Fryer Green Bean Fries

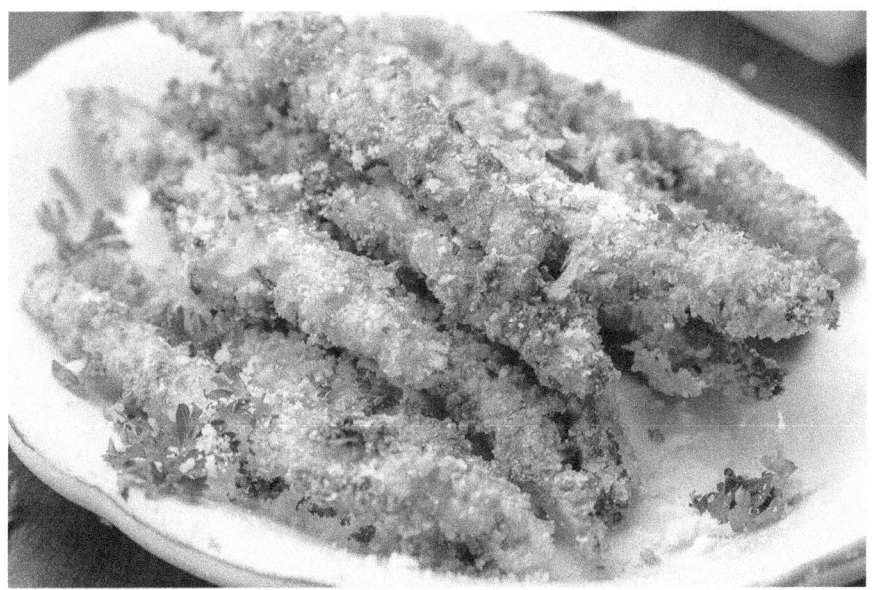

Ingredients

prep: 10 mins
cook: 5 mins
total: 15 mins
Servings: 4

- 1 Pound Fresh Green Beans
- 1 Cup Panko Bread Crumbs
- 1/2 Cup Parm Cheese
- 1 Tbs Garlic Powder
- 2 Eggs
- 1/2 Cup Flour

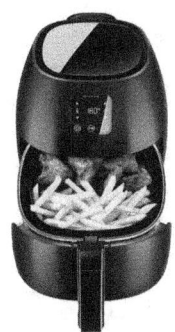

Directions

1. Rinse green beans
2. Coat in flour (Optional)
3. Whisk eggs and dip green beans in eggs
4. Mix together parm cheese, panko bread crumbs and garlic powder
5. after dipping the beans in eggs Dip green beans in panko mix coat the green beans well.
6. Place in air fryer on 390 for 5 minutes or until golden brown.
7. Sprinkle with additional parm cheese

Air-Fryer Stuffed Mushrooms

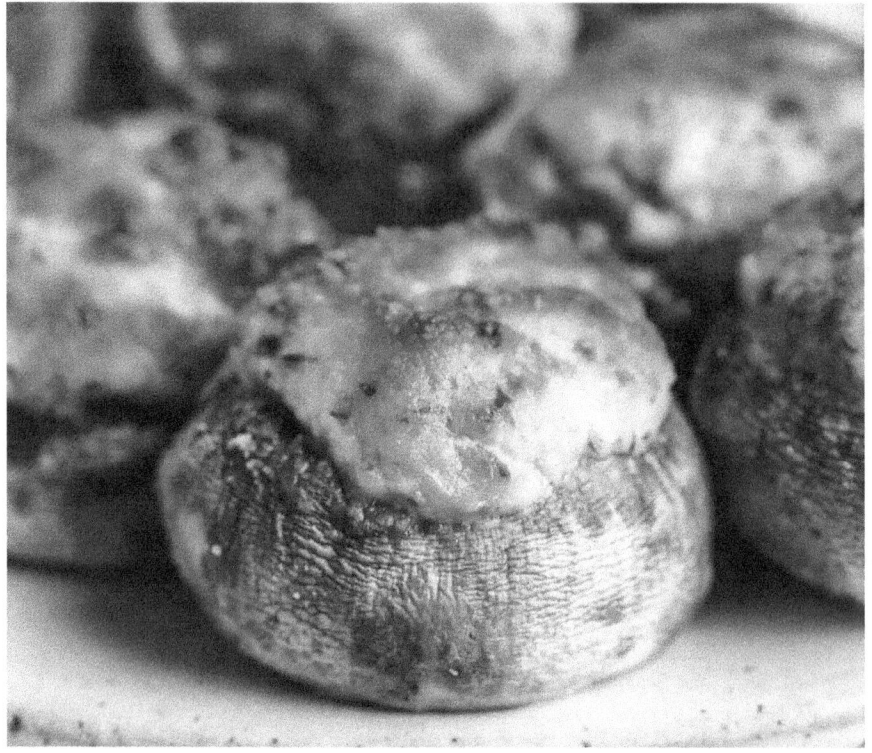

Ingredients

- 1 Lb. Button Mushrooms
- 1 Tbsp. Unsalted Butter
- 1 Garlic Clove, Minced
- 2 Tbsp. Plain Breadcrumbs
- 1/3 Cup Parmesan Cheese
- 1/4 Cup Cream Cheese
- 1/2 Tbsp. Freshly Chopped Parsley
- 1 Tsp. Freshly Chopped Dill
- 1/8 Tsp. Onion Powder

- Prep Time: 15 Minutes
- Cook Time: 10 Minutes
- Total Time: 25 minutes
- Yield: 4 Servings

- 1/8 Tsp. Salt
- 1/4 Cup Panko Breadcrumbs
- 1/4 Cup Shredded Cheese
  (Mozzarella, Cheddar Etc.)
- Cooking Spray Oil

Directions

Remove stems from mushrooms. Shred stems using grater. Melt the butter in a frying pan. Add stems and cook for 2 minutes. Add garlic and plain bread crumbs and cook for a few seconds. In a medium bowl mix cooked stems, Parmesan cheese, cream cheese, parsley, dill, onion powder, and salt. Using a small spoon stuff each mushroom with the stuffing. Set aside. In a separate bowl mix panko breadcrumbs with shredded cheese. Top each mushroom with the topping. Spray with cooking oil. Place mushrooms into the air fryer on the rack, set the timer for 10 minutes and temperature for 360°F.

Crispy Air-Fryer Sweet Potato Wedges

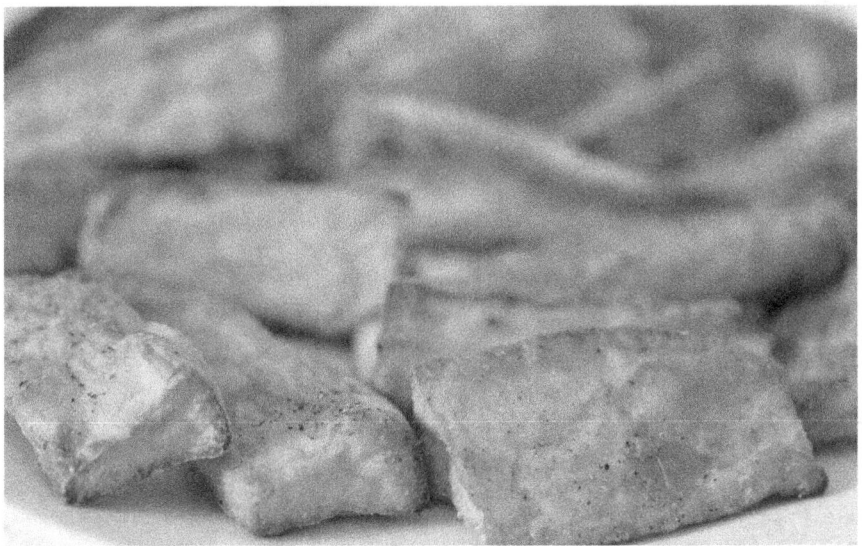

Ingredients

- 1/2 Teaspoon Paprika
- 1/4 Teaspoon Ground Cumin
- 1/4 Teaspoon Black Pepper
- 1/8 Teaspoon Kosher Salt
- 1/8 Teaspoon Ground Coriander
- 1/8 Teaspoon Garlic Powder
- 1 (9-Oz.) Sweet Potato, Cut Lengthwise Into 8 Wedges
- 1 Teaspoon Canola Oil
- 1 Tablespoon Fresh Cilantro Leaves
- 2 Lime Wedges

Course: Appetizer
Cuisine: Southern
Prep Time: 20 minutes
Cook Time: 10 minutes
Total Time: 30 minutes
Servings: 2

Directions

1 - You definitely want to be careful not to burn the fries. I love how easy it is to keep an eye on things with an air fryer. It is also just as easy to put the tray back in and cook a little longer. So use your common sense and sound judgement, and cook those fries to your liking.

2- Don't overcrowd the fryer basket. This recipe makes 2 servings, and this should work for most air fryers without issue. If you want to make more, though, you'll need to cook these in batches. When everything is cooked, you can dump everything back in the sir fryer basket for another minute or so to re-heat, just prior to serving.

3- Commit to your preferred fry size, and cut everything close to the same size. If you vary from this recipe, you may need to adjust cook time. E.g., skinnier fries need to cook less time, thicker fries need more time.

Air-Fryer Twice Baked Potatoes

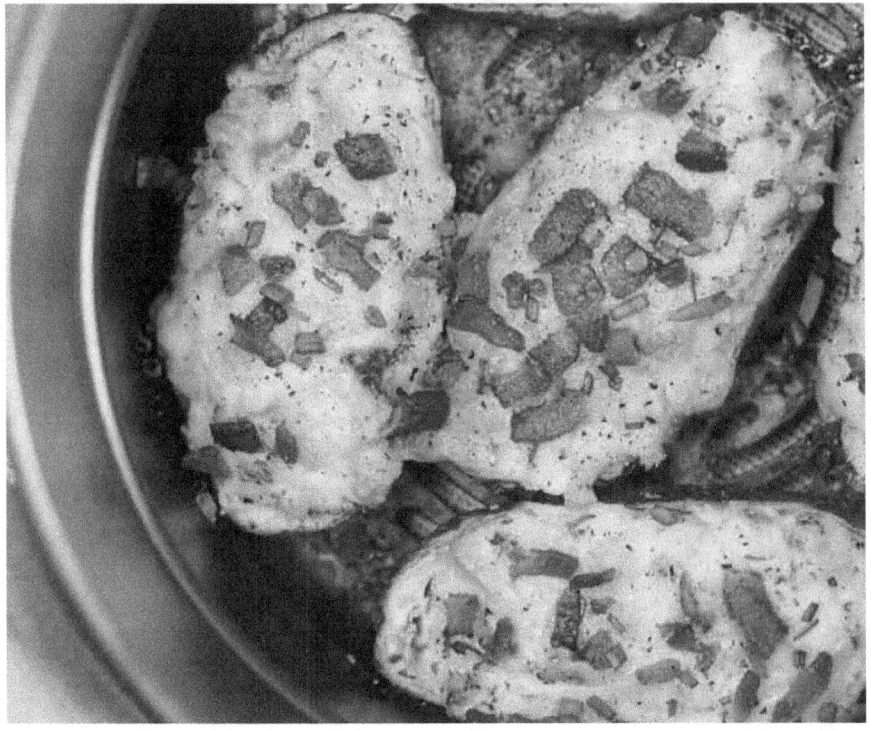

Ingredients

- 2 Cooked Baked Potatoes
- 2 Tablespoon Sour Cream
- 1/2 Cup Cheddar Cheese
- 1 Tablespoon Butter
- 2 Slices Bacon, Cooked

Prep Time: 10 minutes
Cook Time: 15 minutes
Total Time: 25 minutes
Servings: 4

Directions

- Poke three holes into the top of each of the potatoes using a fork.
- Place the potatoes in the air fryer. Cook for 40 minutes on 390 degrees.
- Remove the potatoes from the air fryer and allow them cool.
- Slice each of the potatoes in half lengthwise.
- Add the butter, shredded cheddar cheese, and salt and pepper to taste.
- Top with sour cream, crumbled Butcher Box Bacon, green onions, and chives.

Hearty baked potatoes are filled with mashed potatoes, sour cream and cheese and topped with bacon
...

Air-Fryer Fried Green Tomatoes

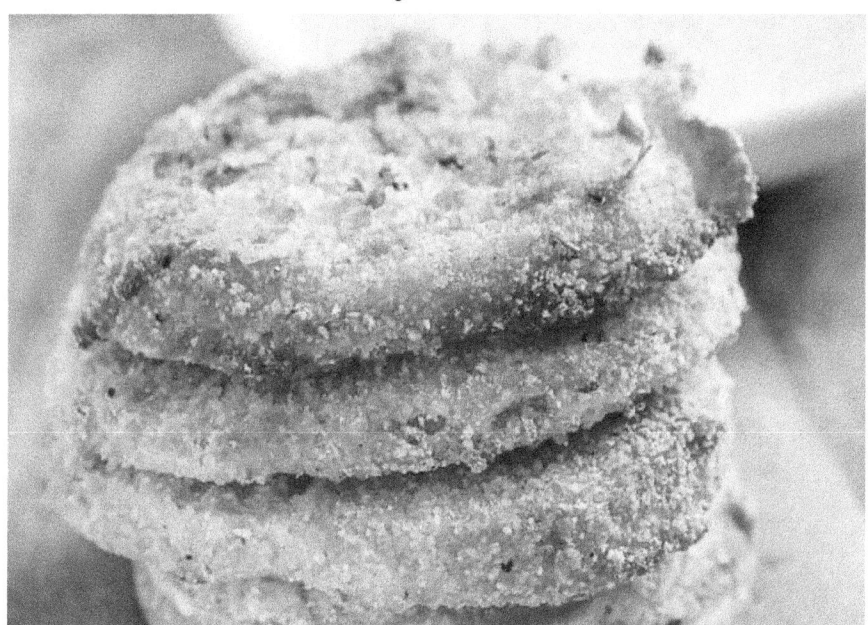

Ingredients

- 2 Green Tomatoes, (3 If They Are Smaller)
- Salt And Pepper
- 1/2 Cup All-Purpose Flour
- 2 Large Eggs
- 1/2 Cup Buttermilk
- 1 Cup Panko Crumbs
- 1 Cup Yellow Cornmeal
- Olive Oil or Vegetable Oil

Course: Appetizer
Cuisine: Southern
Prep Time: 5 minutes
Cook Time: 8 minutes
Total Time: 13 minutes
Servings: 4

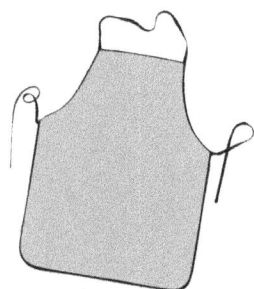

Directions

1. Cut tomatoes into 1/4-inch slices. Pat dry with paper towels and season well with salt and pepper.
2. Place flour in a shallow dish or pie plate, or for easy clean-up use a paper plate.
3. Whisk together eggs and buttermilk in a shallow dish or bowl.
4. Combine Panko crumbs and cornmeal in a shallow dish or pie plate, or for easy clean-up use a paper plate.
5. Preheat air fryer to 400 degrees.
6. Coat the tomato slices in the flour, dip in egg mixture, and then press panko crumb mixture into both sides. Sprinkle a little more salt on them.
7. Mist air fryer basket with oil and place 4 tomato slices in basket. Mist the tops with oil. Air-fry for 5 minutes.
8. Flip tomatoes over, mist with oil and air-fry 3 more minutes.

Air-Fryer Sweet Potatoes

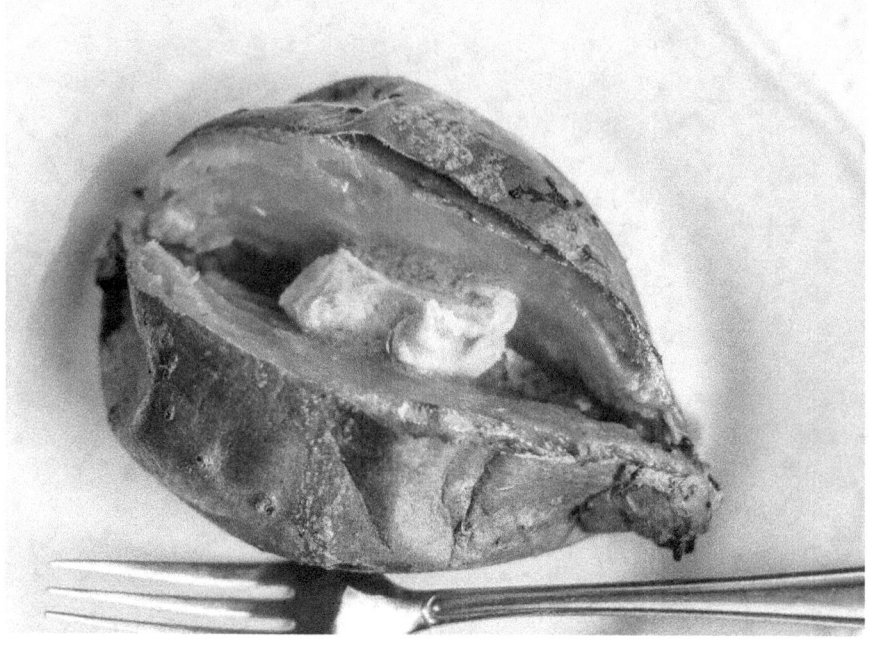

Ingredients

- 2 Medium Size Sweet Potatoes, Washed And Dried
- 1/2 Tablespoon Olive Oil
- Salt
- 1/4 Cup Sugar
- 2 Tablespoons Ground Cinnamon
- 1/2 Teaspoon Butter – Divided

Prep Time: 2 minutes
Cook Time: 45 minutes
Total Time: 47 minutes
Servings: 4

Directions

1. Using a fork, poke several holes in sweet potatoes. Sprinkle over olive oil and salt then rub to coat potatoes. Place in air fryer.
2. Set air fryer temperature to 400 and cook 45 minutes or until fork tender. Remove potatoes from air fryer and let cool for 5 minutes.

1. While potatoes are cooling, mix together sugar and cinnamon. Split potatoes down the middle and sprinkle with desired amount of cinnamon sugar. (Store remaining sugar mixture for future use.) Top with butter and serve.

Oven Baking Instructions
1. Using a fork, poke several holes in sweet potatoes. Sprinkle over olive oil and salt then rub to coat potatoes. Place on a baking sheet. Set oven to 400 degrees and bake for 45 minutes or until potatoes are fork tender.

Air-Fryer Blooming Onion

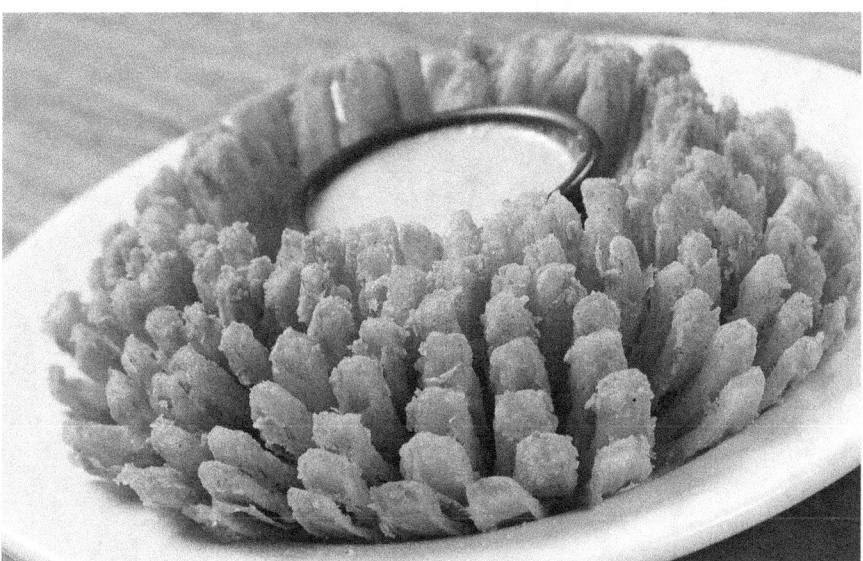

Ingredients

- 1 White Onion (Large)
- 2 Eggs (Large)
- 0.25 Cup Milk
- 1 Tsp Sea Salt
- 0.75 Cup Panko
- 1.5 Tsp Paprika
- 0.5 Tsp Black Pepper
- 1 Tsp Garlic Powder
- 0.5 Tsp Cajun Sauce

Directions

1. Get ready with the coating for the "blooming onion": in one dish, combine olive oil with panko and Cajun sauce; in the second one – combine pepper and salt; in a bowl – mix eggs and milk.

2. Peel onion, cut off the top part and turn it upside down. Moving from ½ inch of the bulb root cut it downwards to the chopping board. Then make more cuts around the bulb until their number is eight leaving some space between them.

3. Pour some ice water into the bowl and dip the sliced onion into it for not less than 2 hours (or for a night at the max). Take bulbs out of water and dry with a paper towel. Weight down the onion "petals" to create the effect of "blooming onion".

4. Mix eggs and the milk (2 tbs), put "flowers" in a large bowl and cover them with egg mixture. Ascertain that the mixture filled in the spaces between "petals". Then turn each "flower" upside down to take away the excess. Cover bulbs with a substance one more time filling in the empty crevices and turn them upside down.
5. Cover "flowers" with panko.

6. Activate the Preheat press, set temperature (360 ˚F) and time for cooking (10 min), and push the Start press.

7. Put "blooming onion" into the basket and cover them with foil.

8. To verify the doneness, check out crispness. If your bulb in blossom is desired to be crispier, continue cooking up to 5 – 10 more minutes.

9. Having reached the desired level of crispness, serve the dish with your favorite sauce (ranch dressing is advisable).

Air-Fryer Stuffed Peppers

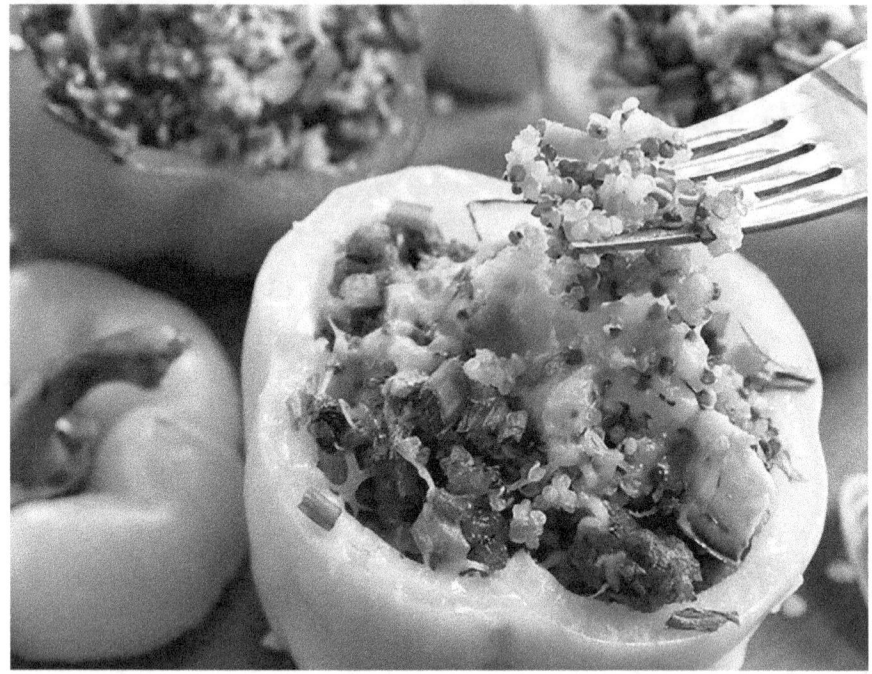

Ingredients

- 6 Green Bell Peppers
- 1 Lb Lean Ground Beef
- 1 Tbsp Olive Oil
- 1/4 Cup Green Onion, Diced
- 1/4 Cup Fresh Parsley
- 1/2 Tsp Ground Sage
- 1/2 Tsp Garlic Salt

- 1 Cup Cooked Rice
- 1 Cup Marinara Sauce, More to Taste
- 1/4 Cup Shredded Mozzarella Cheese

Prep Time: 15 minutes
Cook Time: 18 minutes
Total Time: 33 minutes
Servings: 3-4

Directions

1. Warm up a medium sized skillet with the ground beef and cook until well done.
2. Drain the beef and return to the pan.
3. Add in the olive oil, green onion, parsley, sage, and salt. Mix this well.
4. Add in the cooked rice and marinara, mix well.
5. Cut the top off of each pepper and clean the seeds out.
6. Scoop the mixture into each of the peppers and place in the basket of the air fryer. (I did 4 the first round, 2 the second to make them fit.)
7. Cook for 10 minutes at 355* in the air fryer or air fryer function, carefully open and add cheese.
8. Cook for an additional 5 minutes or until peppers are slightly soft and cheese is melted.
9. Serve.

Air-Fryer Cauliflower Crouton Salad

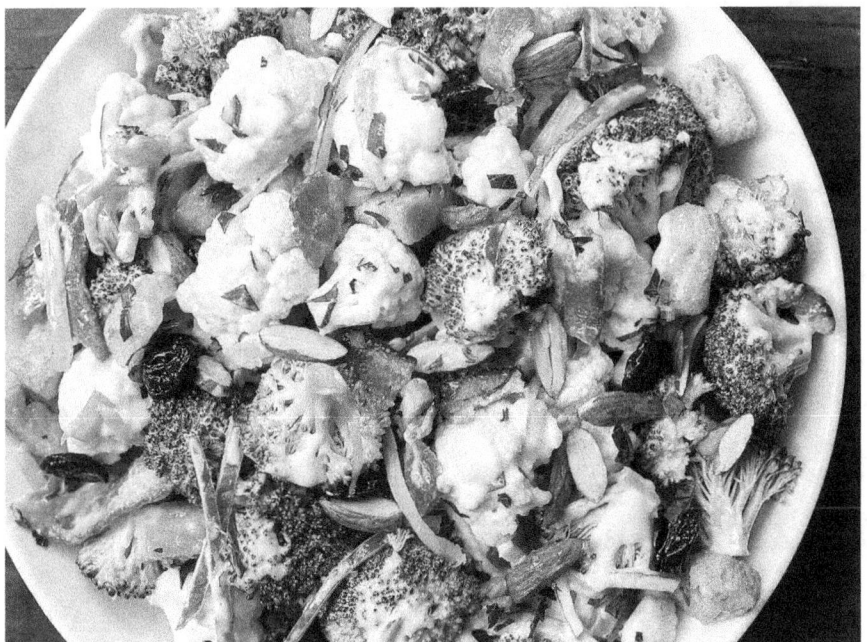

Ingredients

- 1 Small Head Cauliflower, Cut Into Small Bite Sized Florets
- Drizzle Of Olive Oil
- Salt To Taste

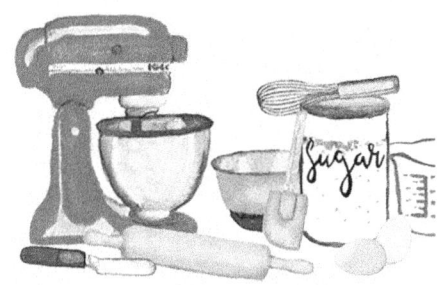

Directions

1. Preheat a Philips Airfryer to 360°F (182°C).
2. Toss cauliflower with olive oil and salt.
3. Arrange the cauliflower in a single layer in the fry basket and insert into the air fryer. Cook for 8 minutes, stirring the cauliflower once halfway through the cooking time. Repeat with any remaining cauliflower.

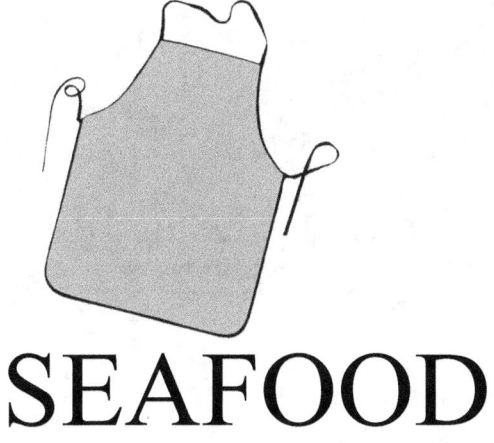

SEAFOOD

Air-Fryer Cajun Shrimp Dinner

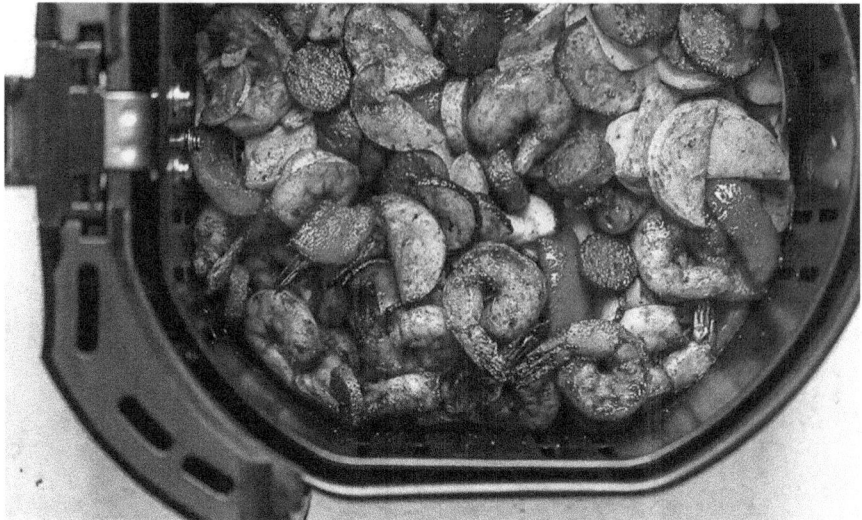

Ingredients

- 1 Tablespoon Cajun Or Creole Seasoning
- 24 (1 Pound) Cleaned And Peeled Extra Jumbo Shrimp
- 6 Ounces Fully Cooked Turkey/Chicken Andouille Sausage, Sliced
- 1 Medium Zucchini, 8 Ounces, Sliced Into 1/4-Inch Thick Half Moons
- 1 Medium Yellow Squash, 8 Ounces, Sliced Into 1/4-Inch Thick Half Moons
- 1 Large Red Bell Pepper, Seeded And Cut Into Thin 1-Inch Pieces
- 1/4 Teaspoon Kosher Salt
- 2 Tablespoons Olive Oil

Directions

1. In a large bowl, combine the Cajun seasoning and shrimp, toss to coat.
2. Add the sausage, zucchini, squash, bell peppers, and salt and toss with the oil.
3. Preheat the air fryer 400F.
4. In 2 batches (for smaller baskets), transfer the shrimp and vegetables to the air fryer basket and cook 8 minutes, shaking the basket 2 to 3 times.
5. Set aside, repeat with remaining shrimp and veggies.
6. Once both batches are cooked, return the first batch to the air fryer and cook 1 minute.

Notes

Tip: Buy shrimp still frozen and defrost as needed. Most shrimp arrives at stores frozen so you may as well buy it frozen and defrost it as needed so it as fresh as possible. To defrost shrimp, thaw overnight in the refrigerator.

Air-Fryer Shrimp

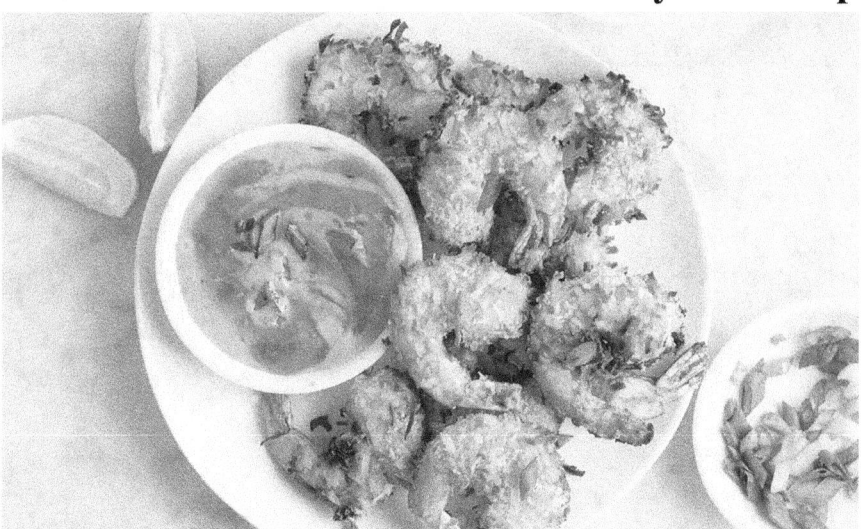

Ingredients

- 1 Pound 21/25 Count Shrimp
  (Peeled And Deveined With Tails Left On)
- 2 Teaspoons Salt (Divided)
- 2 Teaspoons Ground Black Pepper
- 1/4 Cup Flour
- 1/2 Teaspoon Garlic Powder
- 2 Large Eggs
- 1 Teaspoon Soy Sauce
- 1 1/2 Cups Shredded Sweetened Coconut
- 1/2 Cup Panko Breadcrumbs
- Olive Oil Spray

Prep Time: 15 minutes
Cook Time: 16 minutes
Total Time: 31 minutes
Servings: 6
Yield: 18 Shrimp

For the Sauce:

- 1/4 Cup Sweet Chili Sauce
- 1 Tablespoon Apricot Preserves
- 2 Teaspoons Mayonnaise
- Optional: Chopped Scallions, Fresh Lime

Directions

Pat the shrimp dry with paper towels until they are as dry as possible. Salt and pepper generously. In a shallow dish, stir together the flour, garlic powder, and 1/2 teaspoon of the salt and 1/2 teaspoon of the pepper. Dredge the shrimp in the flour, coating both sides. Shake off the excess. In another dish whisk together the eggs and the soy sauce. Dip the flour-coated shrimp in the beaten egg mixture, coating both sides completely so you can't see any flour.

In a third shallow dish, mix the shredded coconut and the panko breadcrumbs together until they are evenly dispersed. Add the rest of the salt and pepper to this mixture. Then dip the shrimp into the coconut mixture. Press the mixture onto the shrimp to help stick as much as possible. Transfer the shrimp to a baking sheet while you continue to bread the rest of the shrimp.

Add the shrimp in an even layer to the bottom of your air fryer. Coat with olive oil spray and cook on 400 F for 8 minutes, flipping them halfway through. You will need to cook them in two batches.

While the shrimp are air frying, prepare the sauce. Whisk together the sweet chili sauce, apricot preserves, and mayonnaise in a small bowl.

Remove the shrimp from the air fryer once they are golden brown. Serve the shrimp with the sauce immediately. Top with chopped scallions and a squeeze of lime juice if you wish.

Air-Fryer Lemon Pepper Shrimp

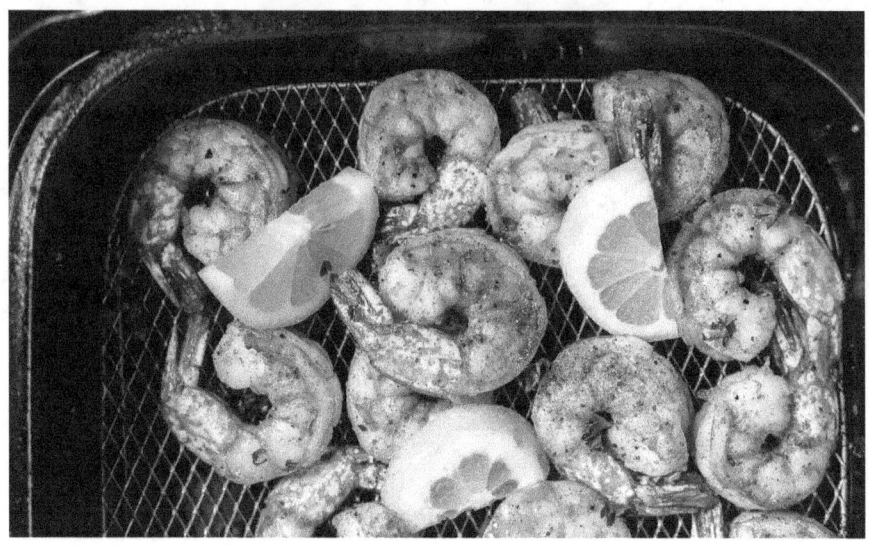

Ingredients

- 1/2 Tablespoon Olive Oil
- 1 Lemon Juiced
- 1 Tsp Lemon Pepper
- ¼ Tsp Paprika
- ¼ Tsp Garlic Powder
- 12 Ounces Uncooked Medium Shrimp Peeled And Deveined
- 1 Lemon Sliced

Course: Main Course
Cuisine: American
Prep Time: 5 minutes
Cook Time:10 minutes
Total Time: 15 minutes
Servings: 2 people

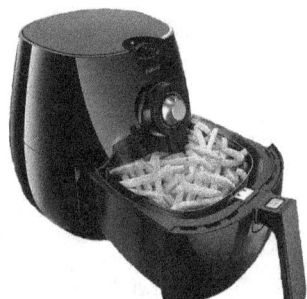

Directions

1. Preheat an air fryer to 400 degrees F
2. Combine olive oil, lemon juice, lemon pepper, paprika, and garlic powder in a bowl.
3. Add shrimp and toss until coated.
4. Place shrimp in the air fryer and cook until pink and firm, 6 to 8 minutes. Serve with lemon slices.
5. For extra flavor you can pour any extra marinade over the shrimp in the air fryer before cooking. This is optional.

Air-Fryer Fish Fillet

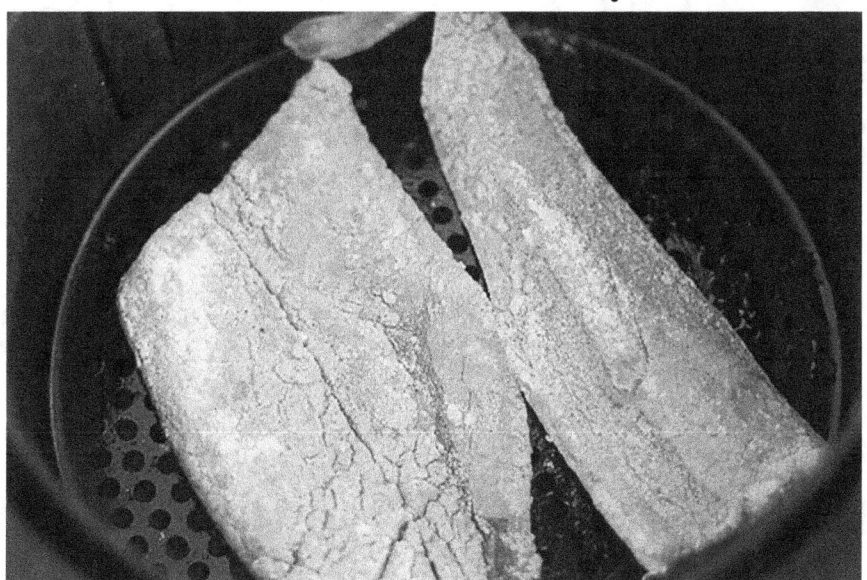

Ingredients

Prep Time: 10 minutes
Cook Time: 14 minutes
Total Time: 24 minutes
Servings: 4

- 4-6 Whiting Fish Fillets Cut In Half
- Oil To Mist

Fish Seasoning

- ¾ Cup Very Fine Cornmeal
- ¼ Cup Flour
- 2 Tsp Old Bay
- 1 ½ Tsp Salt
- 1 Tsp Paprika
- ½ Tsp Garlic Powder
- ½ Tsp Black Pepper
- Your Favorite Fish Seasoning

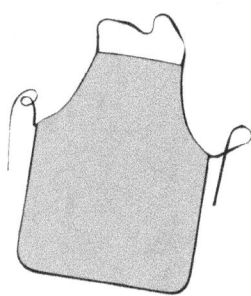

Directions

I normally use fresh fish fillets to make this. But you could also use high-quality frozen fish fillets, just make sure that they're completely defrosted/thawed before you bread and air fry them.

You will need oil to coat the fish fillets before coating in the breading. I usually go for olive oil (love the flavor!), canola, or vegetable oil.

For the breading, use either homemade or store-bought dried bread crumbs. Mix with any spices that you like, onion and garlic powders, black pepper, salt etc

Coat each fish fillet in the seasoning breadcrumbs, and remove any excess breading before you cook in the air fryer.

Air-Fryer Tilapia

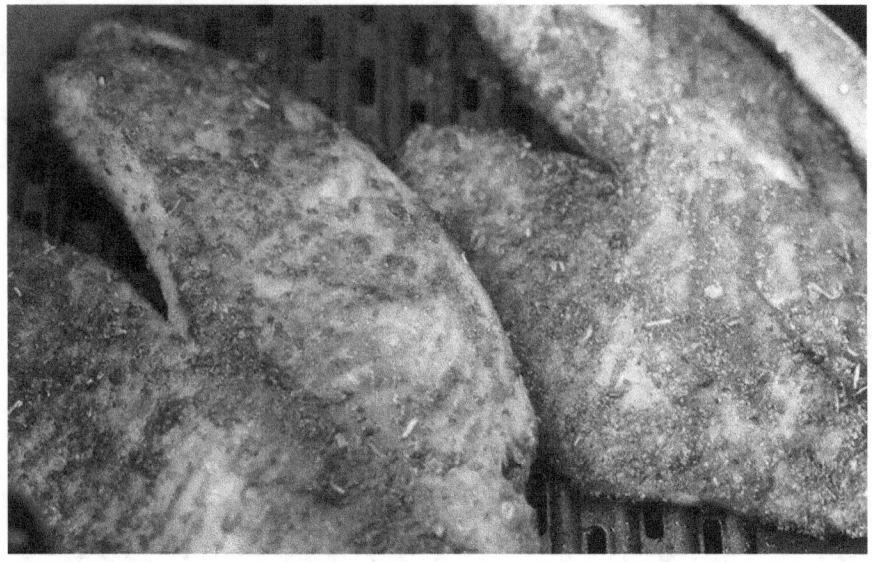

Ingredients

- 4 Tilapia Filets
- 1 Tbsp. Of Your Favorite Seasoning
  (Ex. Garlic Herb, Cajun, Fish Seasoning Blend)
- 1 Tbsp Olive Oil Or Olive Oil Spray
- 1/2 Lemon (Cut In 4 Wedges)

For Serving:

- Tartar Sauce
- Lemon Wedges

Course: Main Course
Cuisine: International
Prep Time: 5 minutes
Cook Time: 15 minutes
Total Time: 20 minutes
Servings: 4
Yield: 4

Directions

If using frozen fish fillets, defrost them. Drizzle with olive oil, and make sure that the fish is well coated with oil. In a shallow dish, mix the bread crumbs with paprika, chili powder, black pepper, garlic powder, onion powder and salt.

Coat each fish fillet in bread crumbs, and transfer to your air fryer basket. Cook in the air fryer at 390°F (200°C) for 12-15 minutes. After the first 8-10 minutes, open the air fryer and flip the fish fillets on the other side then continue cooking.

Notes - You could use either fresh fish fillets or frozen fish fillets that are completely thawed. The fillets should not be too thin as thin strips won't work in this recipe. For smaller pieces of fish, try this Air Fryer fish sticks recipe. Make sure that your air fryer basket is not overcrowded as that will prevent the fish from crisping. You might need to adjust the cooking times depending on the kind and the thickness of the fish that you're using and the model of your air fryer. Fish is ready when it's easily flaked with a fork.

Crispy Air-Fryer Fish Fillets

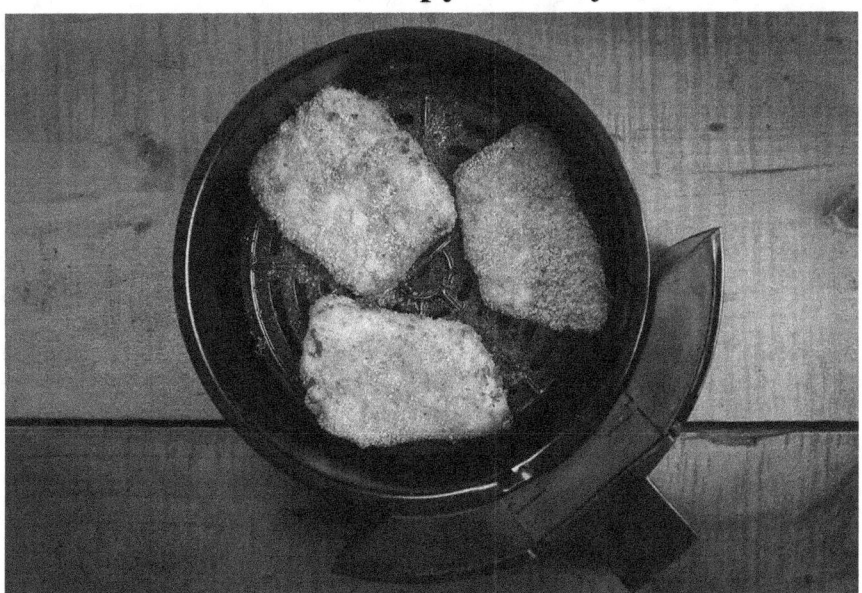

Ingredients

- 8 (28Oz, 800G) Fish Fillets
- 1 Tablespoon Olive Oil Or Vegetable Oil
- 1 Cup (50G) Dry Bread Crumbs
  If Following A Gluten-Free Diet,
  Use Gluten-Free Breadcrumbs.
- ½ Teaspoon Paprika
- ¼ Teaspoon Chili Powder
- ¼ Teaspoon Ground Black Pepper
- ¼ Teaspoon Garlic Powder Or Granules
- ¼ Teaspoon Onion Powder
- ½ Teaspoon Salt

Course: Main Course
Cuisine: American
Prep Time: 5 minutes
Cook Time:15 minutes
Total Time: 20 minutes
Servings: 8

Directions

If using frozen fish fillets, defrost them. Drizzle with olive oil, and make sure that the fish is well coated with oil. In a shallow dish, mix the bread crumbs with paprika, chili powder, black pepper, garlic powder, onion powder and salt. Coat each fish fillet in bread crumbs, and transfer to your air fryer basket. Cook in the air fryer at 390°F (200°C) for 12-15 minutes. After the first 8-10 minutes, open the air fryer and flip the fish fillets on the other side then continue cooking.

These golden fish fillets are cooked in the air fryer until crispy and delicious. Covered in a tasty crust, the fish remains soft and velvety from the inside. Ready in just 20 minutes! Serve air fryer fish with homemade tartar sauce, and lemon wedges

25

Air-Fryer Scallops

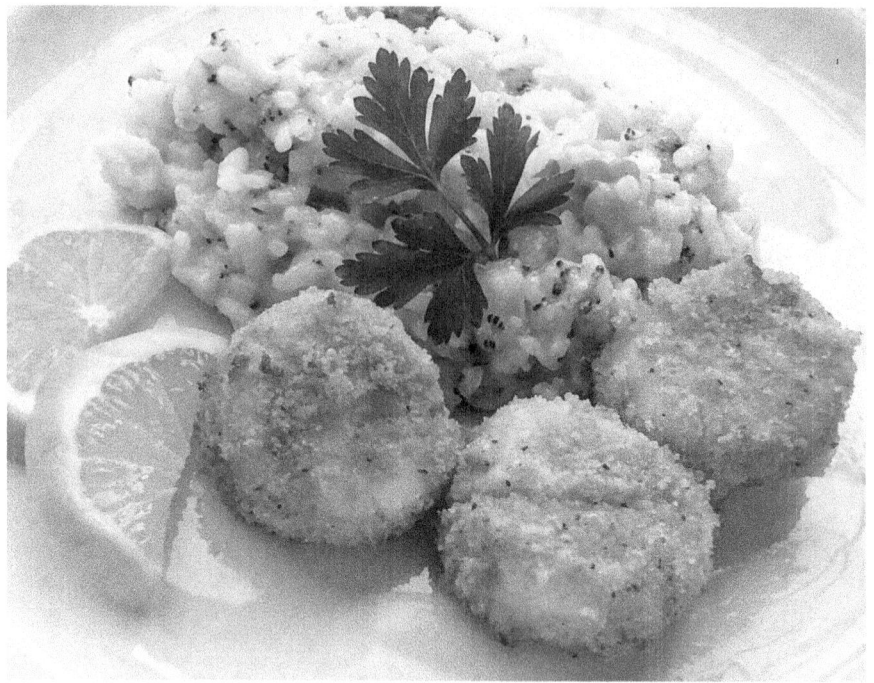

Ingredient

- ½ Cup Finely Crushed Buttery Crackers (Such As Ritz®)
- ½ Teaspoon Garlic Powder
- ½ Teaspoon Seafood Seasoning (Such As Old Bay®)
- 2 Tablespoons Butter, Melted
- 1 Pound Sea Scallops, Patted Dry
- Cooking Spray

Course: Main Course
Cuisine: American
Prep Time: 10 minutes
Cook Time:15minutes
Total Time: 15 minutes
Servings: 4 people

Directions

Step 1 - Preheat the air fryer to 390 degrees F (198 degrees C).

Step 2 - Mix cracker crumbs, garlic powder, and seafood seasoning together in a shallow bowl. Place melted butter in a second shallow bowl.

Step 3 - Dip each scallop in the melted butter and then roll in the breading until completely coated. Set on a plate and repeat with the remaining scallops.

Step 4 - Lightly spray the air fryer basket with cooking spray. Arrange scallops in the prepared basket so that they are not touching each other; you may need to work in batches.

Step 5 - Cook in the preheated air fryer for 2 minutes. Turn scallops over gently with a small spatula and cook until opaque, about 2 more minutes.

Air-Fryer Lobster Tails

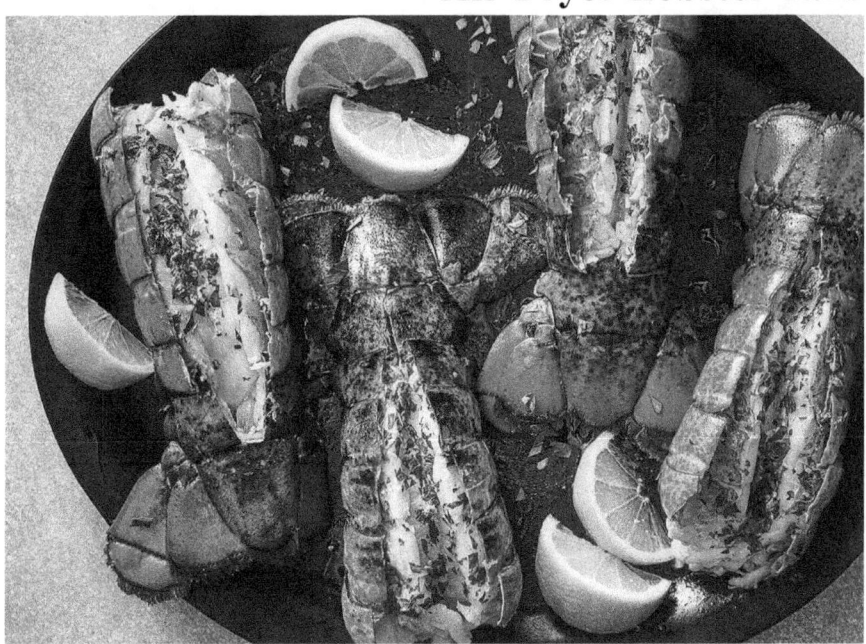

Ingredients

- 2 - 4 Oz. Lobster Tails
- 4 Tbsp. Garlic Butter
- 1/2 Lemon Cut Into Wedges
- Salt & Pepper To Taste
- Chopped Parsley For Garnish (Optional)

Course: Main Course
Cuisine: American
Prep Time: 5 minutes
Cook Time: 8 minutes
Total Time: 13 minutes
Servings: 2 people

Directions

Start your lobster tail recipe by preparing lobster tails. Do this by butterflying the tails. Butterflying means carefully cutting the shell to reveal the lobster meat. Lobster recipes generally call for butterflying the tails, and it's super easy to do!

How to Prepare Lobster Tails

How to butterfly a lobster tail: Butterfly 2 4 oz. lobster tails by using kitchen scissors to cut lengthwise through the center of the shells. Give it a good cut through 3/4 of the lobster, but do not go all of the way through.

Butterflying lobster tails for fried lobster tails

Carefully spread the shell open where you cut. Place your fingers under the meat in the shell and firmly, but gently, pull it out in one piece. Close the shell so that the lobster meat rests on top of the shell.Butterflied lobster tails for fried lobster tails recipe

How to Make Lobster Tails in the Air Fryer

Melt 4 Tbsp. garlic butter sauce over medium heat in a small saucepan. Transfer 2 Tbsp. of the melted butter sauce to a small bowl and brush the lobster tail meat with it.

Season the lobster tails with salt and pepper to your preference. How do you cook lobster tails: Place the lobster tails in the air fryer basket with the cut lobster meat facing up. Cook at 380°F until the lobster meat is opaque, approximately 5 to 7 minutes.

POULTY&MEAT

Air-Fryer Chicken Wings

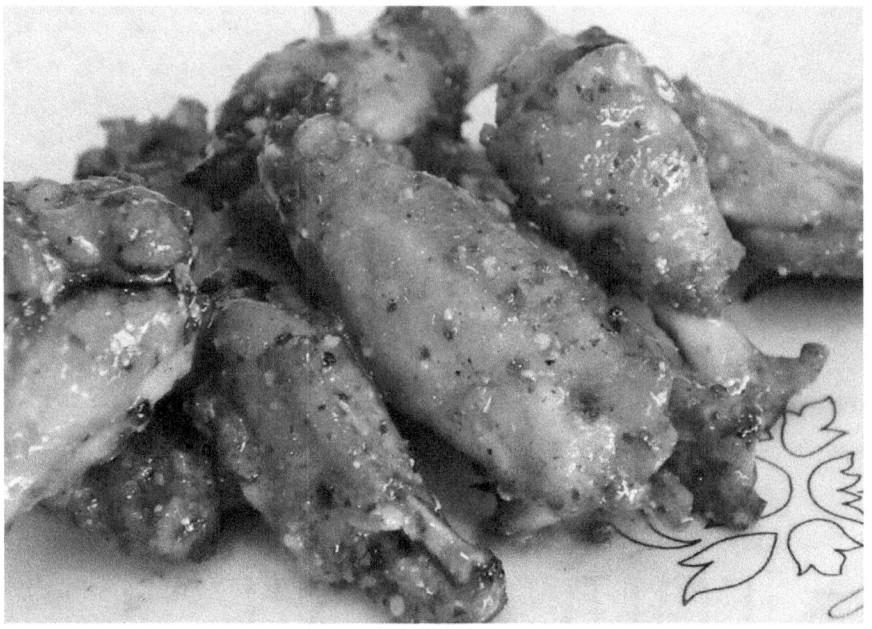

Ingredients

- 1 Lb Chicken Wings – Flats And Drumettes
- 1 Tbsp Olive Oil
- 1 ½ Tsp Garlic Salt
- 1 Tsp Pepper
- ⅛ Tsp Cayenne Pepper

Course:
Cuisine: American
Prep Time: 5 minutes
Cook Time:18 minutes
Total Time: 23 minutes
Servings: 2

Before we begin making air fryer chicken
wings we need to season the meat!

Directions

1. Take the wings and lay them out flat. Pat them dry on both sides with a paper towel. Place them in a large bowl.
2. To the wings in the bowl, add olive oil, garlic salt, pepper, and cayenne pepper. Mix well so every piece is well coated.
3. Place the wings into the air fryer basket and turn it to 380°F. Cook for about 25-30 minutes or until chicken is cooked through. Check the wings every 5-10 minutes or so turning them so they are evenly cooked.
4. Increase the heat to 400°F. and cook for an additional 5-10 minutes to make the skin nice and crispy.
5. Serve them with your choice of dipping sauces and enjoy.

Note: If you have a small air fryer, I would actually not double this recipe, as I've found keeping the wings to one layer is best. If you can double the recipe and still keep the chicken to one layer, adjust the frying time accordingly! Make sure your chicken is thoroughly cooked.

Air-Fryer Fried Chicken Sandwiches

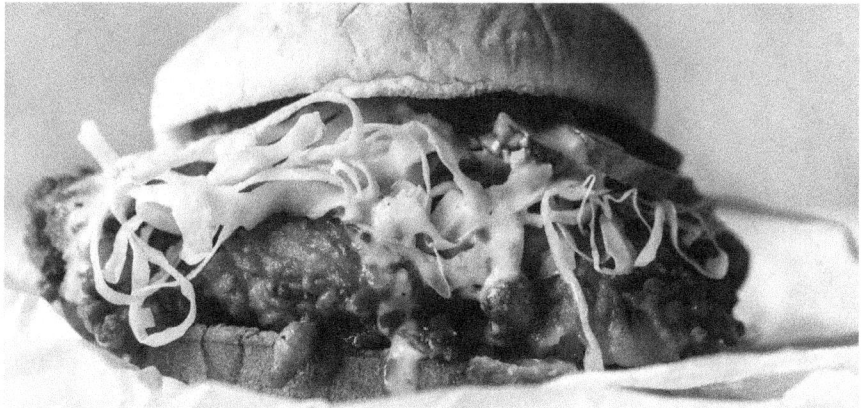

Ingredients

- 2 Chicken Breasts, Halved Crosswise And Cut In Half
- 1/2 Cup Buttermilk, See Tips Above
- 3/4 Cup Panko Breadcrumbs
- 1/2 Cup All-Purpose Flour
- 1/4 Tsp Baking Powder
- 1/2 Tsp Salt
- 1/4 Tsp Dried Oregano
- 1/2 Tsp Paprika
- 1/4 Tsp Garlic Powder
- 1/4 Tsp Dried Thyme
- 1/4 Tsp Ground Ginger
- 1/2 Tsp Ground Black Pepper
- Oil Spray
- 2 Tbsp Butter

Chicken Sauce

- 1/3 Cup Mayonnaise
- 1 Tbsp Honey
- 1 Tbsp Dijon Mustard
- 2 Tsp Yellow Mustard
- 2 Tsp Freshly Squeezed Lime Juice
- Tbsp Bbq Sauce

Slaw

- 3 Cups Shredded Cabbage
- 2 Tbsp Apple Cider Vinegar
- 1 Tsp Sugar
- 1/4 Tsp Salt
- 1/4 Cup Chicken Sauce

Directions

1. Place the halved chicken breasts in a ziplock bag and pour the buttermilk into the bag. Squeeze the air out and seal the bag. Let marinate in the refrigerator for 30 minutes minimum up to several hours.
2. In a shallow bowl combine the panko breadcrumbs, flour, baking powder, and spices.
3. Remove the chicken breasts from the buttermilk with a fork, shake off excess buttermilk, and dredge in the bread-crumb mixture to coat on all sides. Spray with oil spray from both sides.
4. Put the chicken breasts in one layer in the Airfryer basket and air fry at 375F (190C) for 10-12 minutes in total until internal temperature reads 175F (79C) and the chicken breasts are golden brown and crispy. Flip the chicken with a fork or cookie spatula after 5 minutes and spray with more oil if needed.
5. While the chicken is cooking, make the chicken sauce by combining all the ingredients in a bowl. Then make the slaw by combining shredded cabbage, vinegar, sugar and salt in another bowl. Let the slaw sit for 2 minutes then add 1/4 cup of the sauce you made before and stir until combined.
6. Then brush the cut sides of the Sandwich Rolls with butter and heat a large skillet over medium heat. Toast rolls buttered side down until browned and crisp, about 1 minute.
7. To assemble the sandwiches, spread some sauce on the bottom roll, place a fried chicken breast on top, and top with slaw.

Air-Fryer Pork Chops

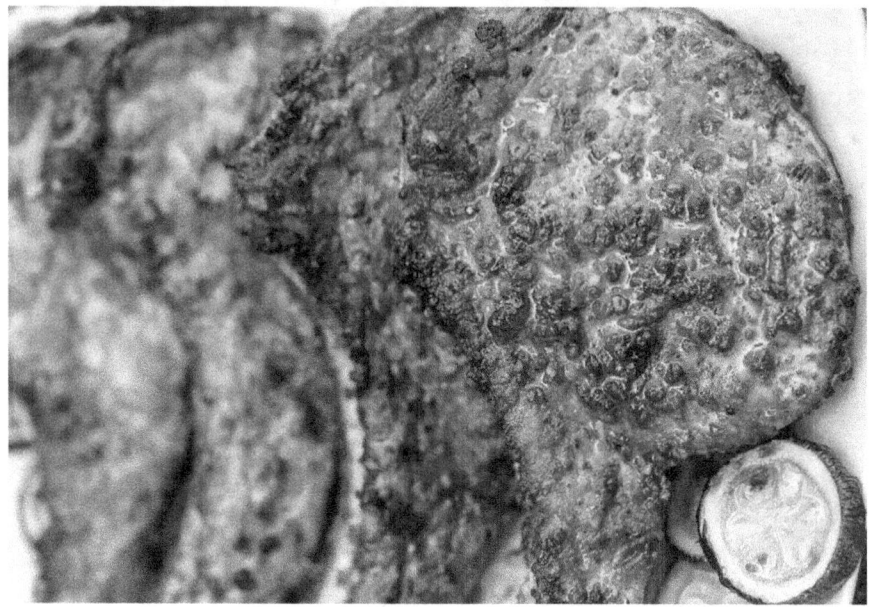

Ingredients

- 4 Bone-In Pork Chops
- 2 Tablespoons Extra-Virgin Olive Oil
- 1/2 Cup Freshly Grated Parmesan
- 1 Teaspoon Kosher Salt
- 1 Teaspoon Smoked Paprika
- 2 Teaspoons Garlic Powder
- 1 Teaspoon Onion Powder
- 1 Teaspoon Ground Mustard
- 1/2 Teaspoon Italian Dried Herbs
- 1/2 Teaspoon Freshly Ground Black Pepper

Course:
Cuisine: American
Prep Time: 15 minutes
Cook Time: 15 minutes
Resting Time 5 minutes
Total Time: 35 minutes
Servings: 4

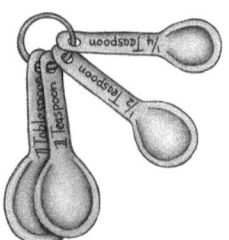

Directions

1. Pat dry pork chops with paper towels, then brush both sides with oil.

2. In a medium bowl, combine all the Seasoning ingredients, stir to combine.

3. Coat both sides of pork chops with the Parmesan mixture, pressing slightly for it to stick to the chops.

4. Place pork chops in the basket of the air fryer and cook at 400° for 12 minutes,
flip pork chops after 6 minutes.

5. The pork chops should be golden brown and cooked to an internal temperature of
145-160 degrees Fahrenheit.

6. Arrange on a serving plate and let them rest 10 minutes before slicing or serving.

Air-Fryer Bacon and Egg Bite Cups

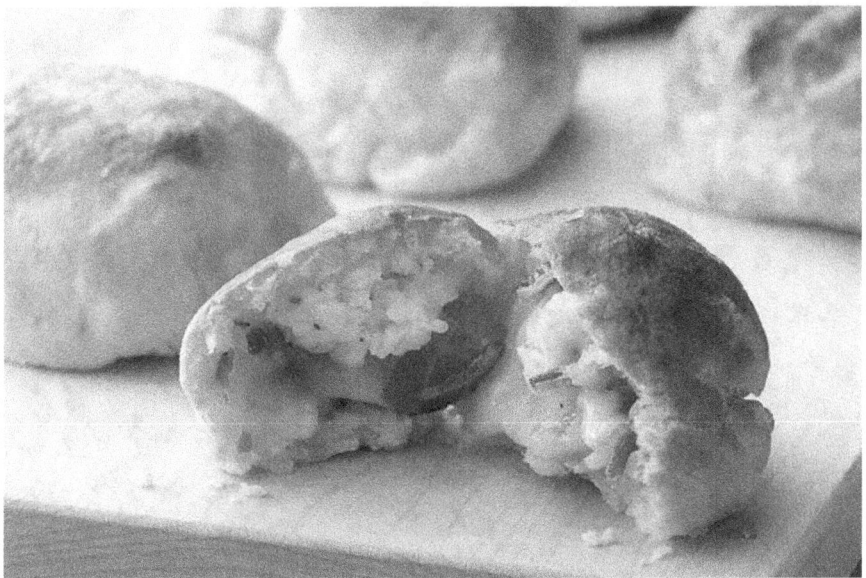

Ingredients

- 6 Large Eggs
- 2 Tablespoons Of Heavy Whipping Cream Or Milk (Any Is Fine)
- Salt And Pepper To Taste
- ¼ Cup Chopped Green Peppers
- ¼ Cup Chopped Red Peppers

Course:
Cuisine: American
Prep Time: 5 minutes
Cook Time:15 minutes
Total Time: 20 minutes
Servings: 4

Directions

1. Spray the inside of cups of silicone mold thoroughly with a cooking spray.
2. Add the chopped green onions and ham (if using) and put the silicone mold in the air fryer basket.
3. Cook these toppings in the air fryer at 360F for 3 minutes.
4. Meanwhile, in a large measuring cup with a pouring spout, combine the eggs, milk, salt and pepper.
5. When the toppings are done cooking, take the basket out of the air fryer. Carefully pour the egg mixture into the egg bites mold cups over the toppings. Top the egg bites with shredded cheese.
6. Cook the egg bites in the air fryer at 360F for 12 minutes, or until the eggs are set.

Notes
Do not use the cover that comes with the egg mold in the air fryer, the egg bites should be baked uncovered.

Air-Fryer Bacon

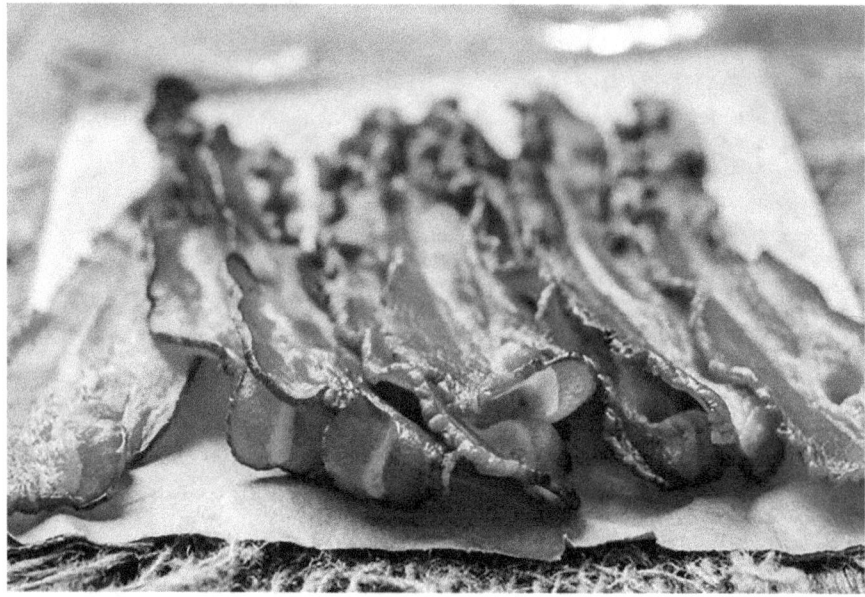

Ingredients

- 2-8 slices bacon depending on your air fryer basket size
- Regular or Sprinkle (Light) Cinnamon Sugar after cooked

Course: Basics, Breakfast
Cuisine: American
Prep Time: 4 minutes
Cook Time: 11 minutes
Total Time: 15 minutes
Servings: 11 slices

Directions

1. Lay bacon inside air fryer basket in a single layer.
2. Set air fryer to 400° and cook until crispy, about 10 minutes. (You can check halfway through and rearrange slices with tongs.)

Problems with cooking bacon in the air fryer?
The only problem we can think of is that if you cook too much bacon at once at a higher temp, you might get some smoking. Make sure to have the air fryer in a well ventilated kitchen or under the vent hood. It is more contained then when you pan fry the bacon, but the air fryer will still emit bacon steam. And only other issue is that if you walk away or don't flip the bacon, you might get burned bacon.

Making brown sugar air fryer fried bacon is a probably the fastest, cleanest, most delicious way I've ever made bacon, and now since I've done it, I don't think I'll ever go back to the oven or stovetop method. And you can quote me on that!

Tips for Making Air Fryer Bacon
- Use strips that are uniform in size and have an equal ratio of fat to meat.
- If the strips are too long, cut them in half and fry in batches.
- Once all the bacon is done cooking, put the whole batch back in the air fryer for 1 minute so it's all warm and crispy!

Air-Fryer Steak

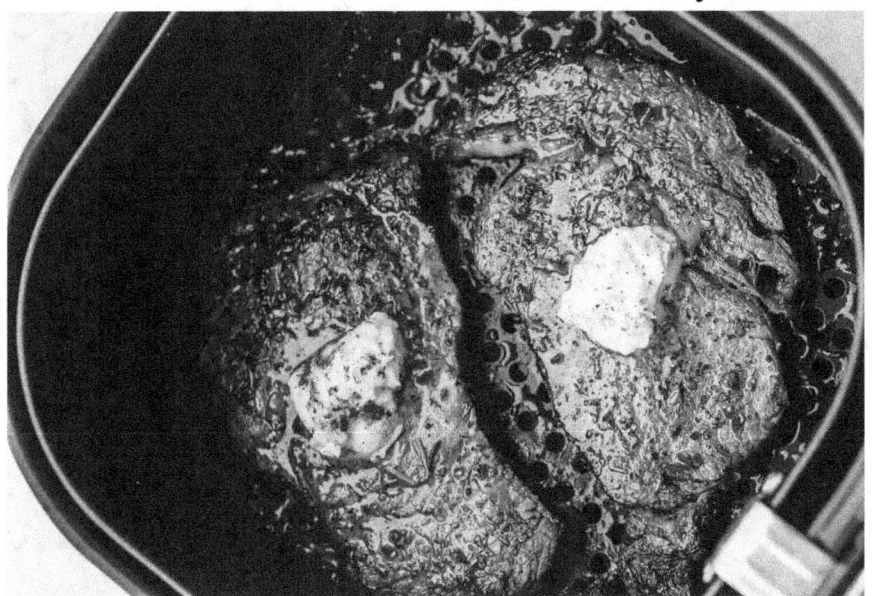

Ingredients

- 2 6 Oz. Beef Tenderloin Filet Mignon Steaks
- 2 Tbsp. Chicago Steak Seasoning
  Or Seasoning Of Your Choice
  (Just Salt & Pepper Works Well Also)
- 2 Tbsp. Garlic Butter
- 2 Tbsp. Olive Oil

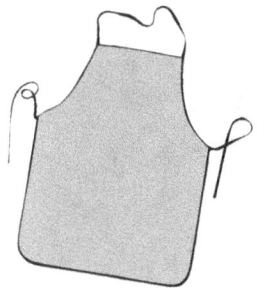

Directions

1. Remove the steak from the fridge and pat dry (preferably let it sit out until it is room temperature).
2. Brush (or spray) the top of the sirloin with cooking fat (about 1-2 tsp.) and season generously.
3. Coat the bottom of the air fryer basket in cooking fat and add the sirloin steak to the basket.
4. Cook for 15 minutes.
5. Flip the sirloin steak and cook an additional 5 minutes.
6. Remove the steak from the air fryer and let it rest for 5 minutes before slicing and servings.

Air-Fryer Hamburgers

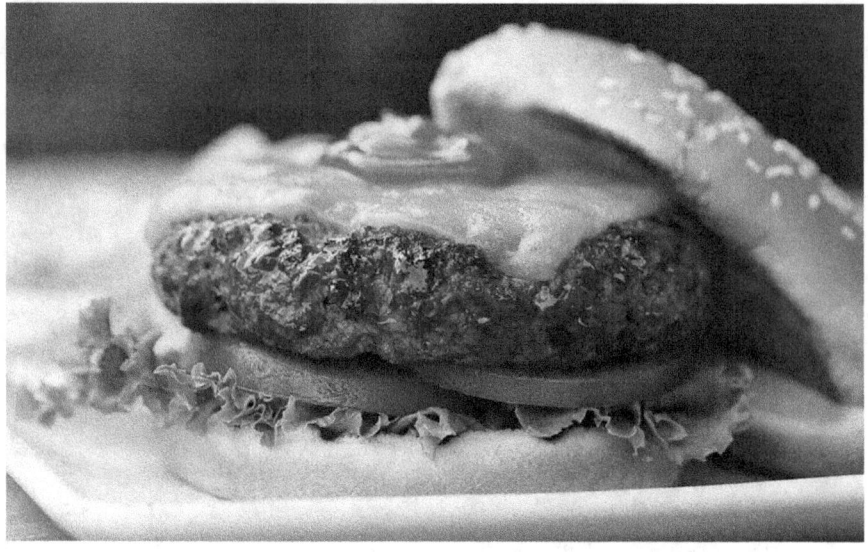

Ingredients

- 1 1 Inch Thick
- Hamburger Patty
- 1 Hamburger Bun (Optional)
- 3 Lettuce Leaves (Optional)
- 2Tbsp Tomato Sauce (Optional)
- 1Slice Cheese (Optional)
- 2Slices Tomato (Optional)

Course:
Cuisine: American
Prep Time: 4 minutes
Cook Time:12-15 minutes
Total Time: 18 minutes
Servings: 1 slices

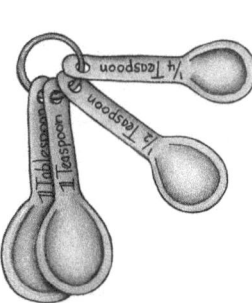

Directions

1. While waiting for the patty to cook, prepare the hamburger ingredients.
2. Once cooked, build your hamburger and enjoy!

Note:
3. Cooking time should be used as a guide only. Thickness of hamburger patty, amount of fat, and how compacted the patty is will determine the cooking time. I recommend using an instant cooking thermometer to check on the progress. This is based on slightly thicker than 1 inch thick and being well done.

Air-Fryer Crispy Pork Belly

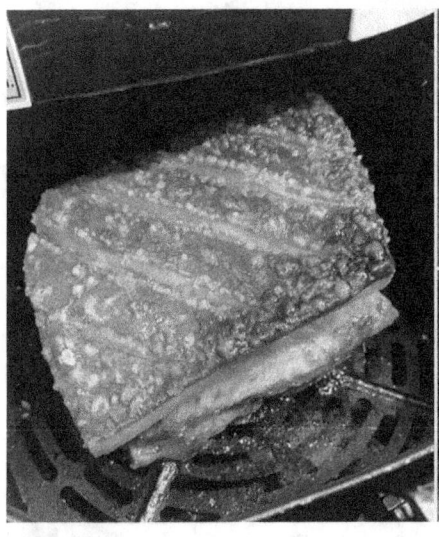
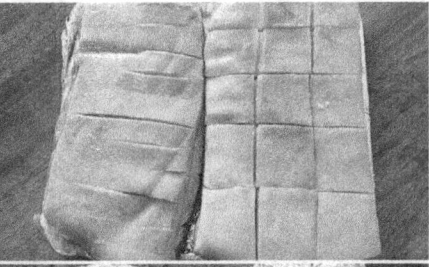
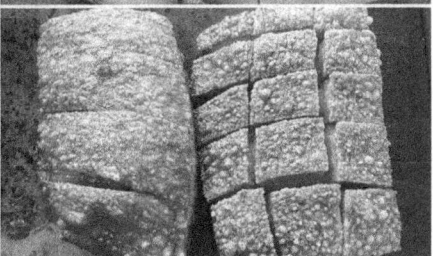

Ingredients

- 1Kg Pork Belly
- 3Tsp Salt
- 2Tsp Sugar
- 1/2Tsp Five-Spice Powder

Course:
Cuisine: American
Prep Time: 15 minutes
Cook Time:30 minutes
Total Time: 45 minutes
Servings: 1 slices

Directions

1. Use a knife to scrape any impurities from the pork belly, rinse thoroughly and set aside.
2. Combine the Salt, Sugar, and Five-Spice powder and set aside.
3. Blanch (boil) pork belly in boiling water for around 15 minutes, or until it's around 60% to 70% done
4. Drain the Pork Belly well of excess water, and pat it dry.
5. Cut a few slits in the meat (not the Rind side) so that the seasoning can be well distributed.
6. Coat the meat with seasonings evenly. Make sure there's no seasoning on the rind
7. Turn over and wipe dry the Rind.
8. Using a metal skewer, poke as many little holes as possible in the rind. Not too deep.
9. Wrap the Pork Belly meat in aluminum foil but leave the rind unwrapped.
10. Place in the fridge, and let it air dry overnight.

COOKING

- Remove from the fridge and let it rest at room temperature for a short while.
- Using a metal skewer, once again, poke some holes in the rind.
- Place the pork belly with the rind facing up into the air-fryer.
- Cook for around 20 minutes
- Remove from the air fryer and pat dry the Rind once again.
- Place back in the air fryer and continue cooking for around 25 minutes

RECIPE NOTES

- Cook from Room Temperature
- As thickness and hardness of the pork belly and rind varies, you may need to add a little extra time at the end.

Air-Fryer Rack of Lamb

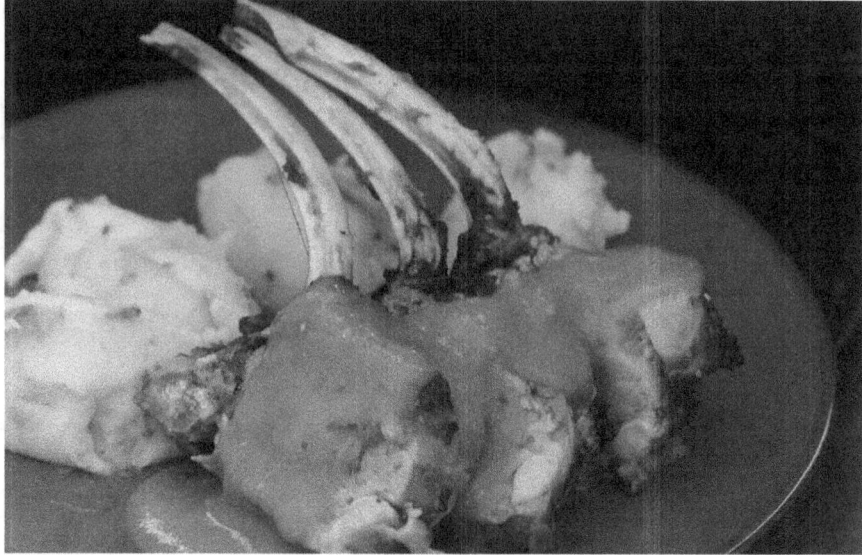

Ingredients

- 1 Rack Of Lamb
- 2 Tablespoons Dried Rosemary
- 1 Tablespoon Dried Thyme
- 2 Teaspoons Minced Garlic
- Salt
- Pepper
- 4 Tablespoons Olive Oil

Course:
Cuisine: American
Prep Time: 5 minutes
Cook Time:15 minutes
Total Time: 20 minutes
Servings: 4

Directions

1. Start by making your mixture of herbs, mix in a small bowl, the rosemary, thyme, garlic, salt, pepper, and olive oil.Combine well.
2. Then rub the mixture all over the lamb.
3. Place the rack of lamb into the air fryer.
4. Note: Depending on how big your air fryer is, you may have to remove a rib, to make it work.
5. Set the temperature to 360 degrees F, for 10 minutes.
6. After 10 minutes, measure your internal temperature of the rack of lamb by using the method above.
7. If you want rare it would be 145 degrees F.
8. If you want medium it would be 160 degrees F.
9. If you want well done, it would be 17.0 degrees F.Note: The USDA does recommend cooking all lamb products to 160 degrees F.
10. Then remove, plate and serve.

Keywords: air fryer lamb chop recipes lamb chops air fryer time air fryer lamb chops recipe for rack of lamb in air fryer air fryer lamb breast rack of lamb recipe air fryer boneless leg of lamb leg of lamb steak air fryer
Did you make this recipe?

Air-Fryer Spicy Lamb Sirloin Steaks

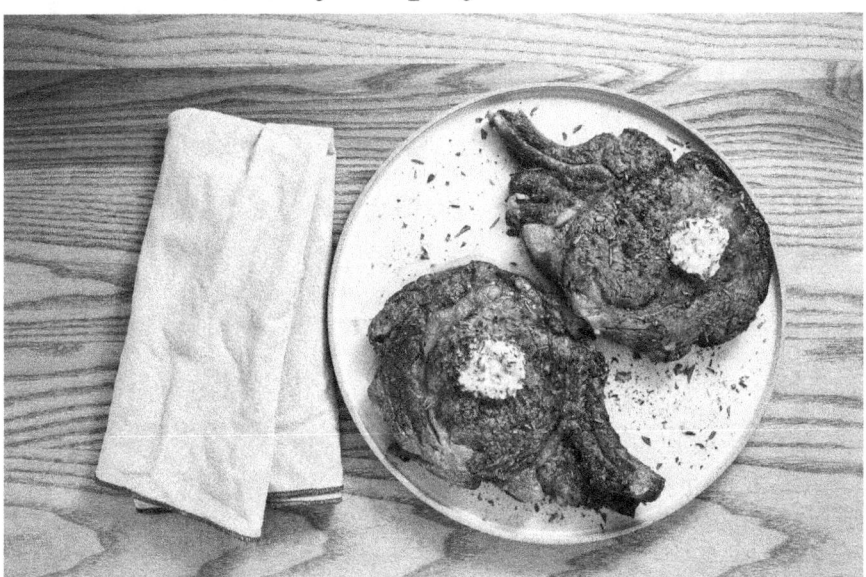

Ingredients

- 1/2 Onion
- 4 Slices Ginger
- 5 Cloves Garlic
- 1 Teaspoon Garam Masala
- 1 Teaspoon Ground Fennel
- 1 Teaspoon Ground Cinnamon
- 1/2 Teaspoon Ground Cardamom
- 1/2 - 1 Teaspoon Cayenne Pepper
- 1 Teaspoon Kosher Salt
- 1 Pound Boneless Lamb Sirloin Steaks

Course:
Cuisine: Indian
Prep Time: 40 minutes
Cook Time:15 minutes
Total Time: 55 minutes
Servings: 4

Directions

1. Into a blender bowl, add all ingredients except the lamb chops.
2. Pulse and blend until the onion is minced fine and all ingredients are blended, about 3-4 minutes.
3. Place the lamb chops into a large bowl. Use a knife to slash into the meat and fat to allow the marinade to penetrate better.
4. Add the blended spice paste and mix well.
5. Allow the mixture to rest for 30 minutes or up to 24 hours in a refrigerator.
6. Let your air fryer to 330F for 15 minutes and place the lamb steaks in a single layer in the air fryer basket and cook, flipping half way through.
7. Using a meat thermometer, ensure that the meat has reached an internal temperature of 150F for medium well, and serve.

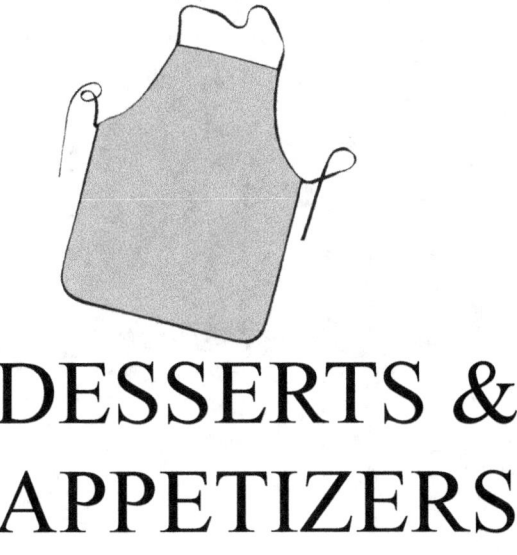

DESSERTS & APPETIZERS

Air-Fryer Fried Oreos

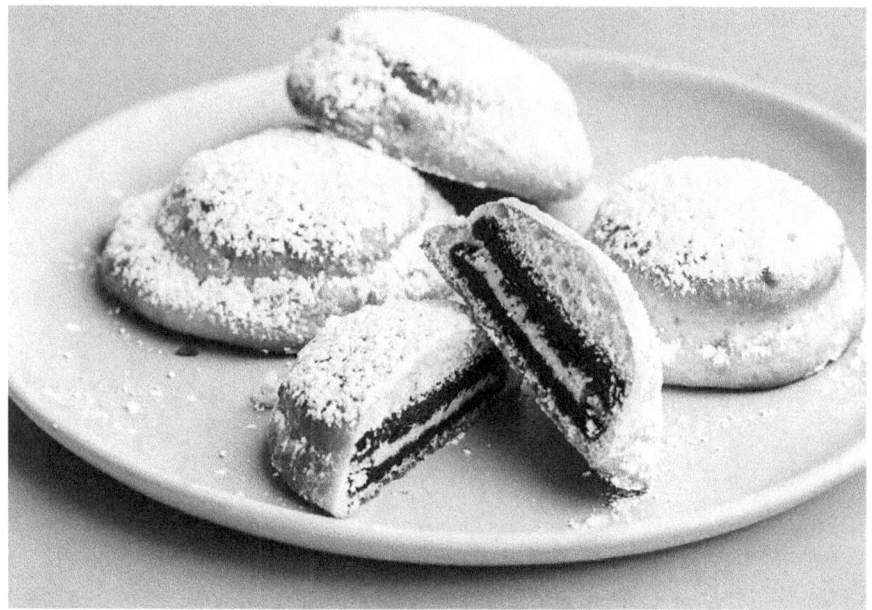

Ingredients

- 8 Oz. Tube Crescent Rolls
- 8 Oreos
- Powdered Sugar For Garnish

Course:
Cuisine: American
Prep Time: 8 minutes
Cook Time:10 minutes
Total Time: 18 minutes
Servings: 8

Directions

1. Cut roll of Crescent rolls into 8 sections.
2. Roll one section into a ball and then flatten it on a nonstick surface into an oval shape.
3. Dip one Oreo in the milk quickly.
4. Place Oreo on flattened dough and fold ends around, covering the Oreo.
5. Make sure all seams are sealed completely.
6. Repeat for remaining Oreos.
7. Preheat air fryer to 375° Fahrenheit for 3 minutes.
8. Air fry 4 Oreos for 4 minutes or until golden brown.
9. Sprinkle with powdered sugar.
10. Repeat steps 7 and 8 with remaining Oreos.

Air-Fryer Cinnamon Rolls

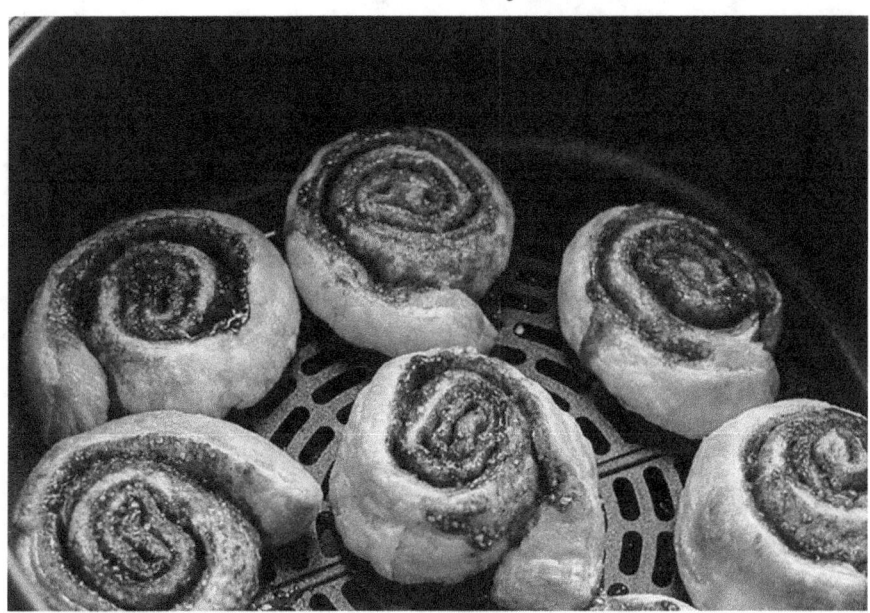

Ingredients

- 1 Tablespoon Ground Cinnamon
- Unsalted Butter At Room Temperature
- 6 Tablespoons Brown Sugar
- 1 Sheet Of Puff Pastry
- ½ Cup Powdered Sugar
- 1 Tablespoon Milk
- 2 Teaspoons Fresh Lemon Juice

Course:
Cuisine: American
Prep Time: 10 minutes
Cook Time: 15 minutes
Total Time: 25 minutes
Servings: 8

Directions

1. Combine cinnamon, butter, and brown sugar in a bowl and mix.
2. Roll out the puff pastry sheet into a rectangular shape and thinly spread the cinnamon mixture over it.
3. Gently roll up the sheet up loosely to form the cinnamon swirls.
4. Cut the roll into 2.5CM long pieces.
5. Place this in a 200°C preheated air fryer and cook for 7 minutes or until golden brown.
6. To make the icing, combine the powdered sugar, lemon juice and milk.
7. Pour icing over the cooked cinnamon rolls and serve warm.

Air-Fryer Cinnamon Roll Cookies

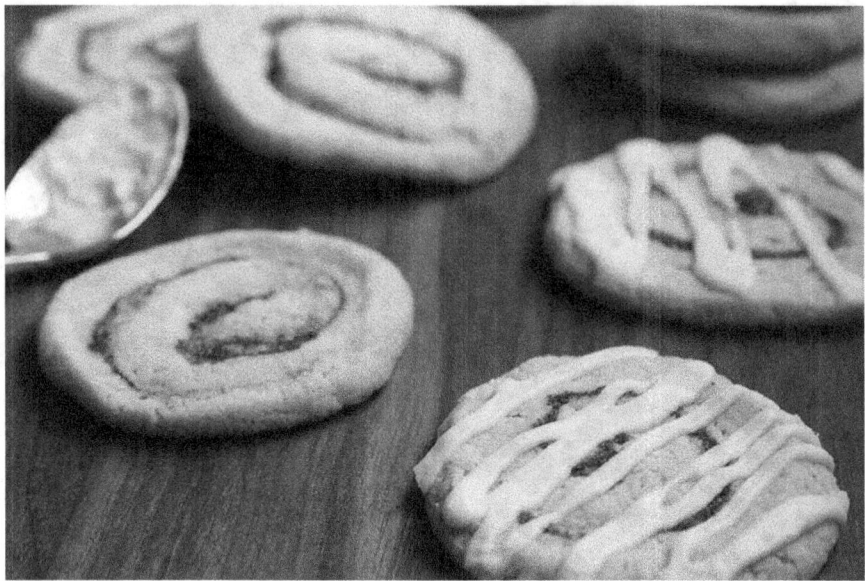

Ingredients

- 1 Pie Crust (Roll, Sold In The Dairy Department)
- 2 Tablespoons Melted Butter
- 1/4 Cup Sugar
- 2 Teaspoon Gorund Cinnamon

Course:
Cuisine: American
Prep Time: 10 minutes
Cook Time:10 minutes
Total Time: 20 minutes
Servings: 15 cookies 1x

Directions

1. Start by laying the pie dough on a flat surface.
2. Use your pizza cutter to make a square. (trim the excess pie dough)
3. In one bowl, add some melted butter.
4. In another bowl, mix together the sugar and ground cinnamon.
5. Use a pastry brush and rub the melted butter on top.
6. Then sprinkle the cinnamon and sugar mixture on top of the butter.
7. Then roll up the dough.
8. Use a sharp knife and cut the pieces about 1/2 inch thick.
9. Place the cookies on the air fryer tray or in the air fryer basket (if you use a basket, you need to line in with parchment paper)

Set the temperature to 320 degrees F, for 6-9 minutes. The exact time will depend on your air fryer. While the cookies are air frying, make the icing. Then let the cookies slightly cool, and then drizzle the icing on top, and sprinkle some of the cinnamon/sugar mixture on top.

Air-Fryer Sweet Potato Chips

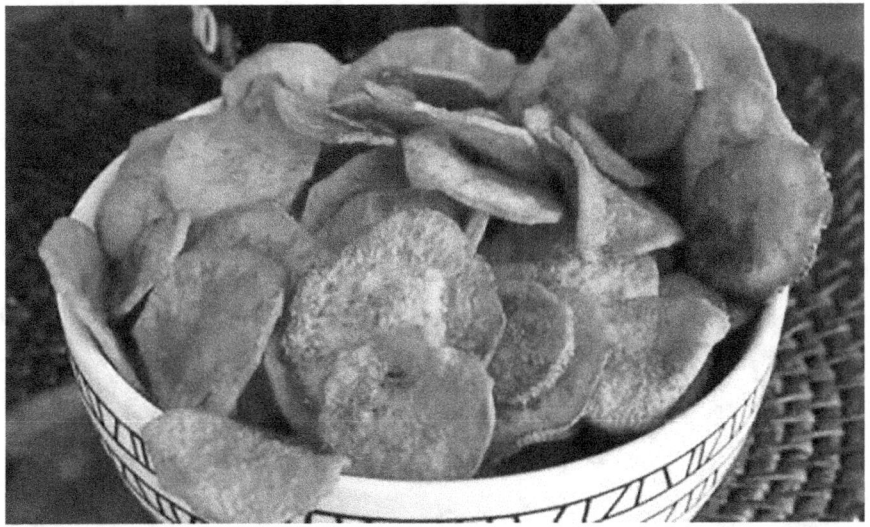

Ingredients

- 1 ½ Cups Sweet Potatoes - 2 Medium Sweet Potatoes
- 1 Tablespoon Extra Virgin Olive Oil
- 2 Tablespoons Organic Brown Sugar Light Or Dark
- 2 Teaspoons Chili Powder
- 1 Teaspoon Ground Cumin
- ½ Teaspoon Salt

Course: Side Dish
Cuisine Snacks
Cuisine: American
Prep Time: 15 minutes
Cook Time: 9 minutes
Total Time: 24 minutes
Servings: 4

Directions

- Thinly slice sweet potatoes.
- Toss in a bowl with the oil so that each sweet potato slice is lightly coated. You can use your hands if you like.
- Mix the brown sugar, chili powder, cumin, and salt in a small bowl.
- If any water has come out of the sweet potatoes while they were sitting then you can drain that off.
- Sprinkle the seasoning mix over the sweet potatoes and toss so that each slice has seasoning on it. They are lightly coated as in the photo above.
- Lay sweet potatoes in a single layer in the air fryer touching or overlapping a tiny bit. If you have a stirring arm in your air fryer that has to be removed.
- Shake the basket halfway through or lightly stir to get them off the bottom of the air fryer bottom.
- When done remove chips to a cooling rack and let them cool. They will get crispier as they cool.
- Done and eat or store in an airtight container.

Air-Fryer French Fries

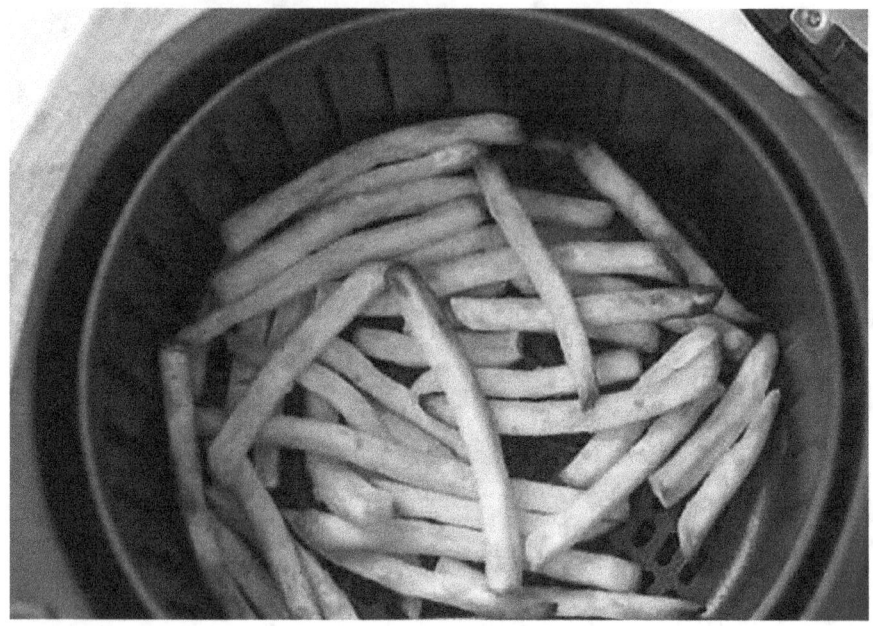

Ingredients

- 1 Pound Yukon Gold Or Russet Potatoes
  (Peeled And Sliced Into 1/2-Inch Thick Sticks)
- 1 Tablespoon Extra Virgin Olive Oil
- Salt And Pepper (To Taste)
- 1 Tablespoon Flat Leaf Parsley (Finely Chopped) Optional

Course:
Cuisine: American
Prep Time: 5 minutes
Cook Time: 15 minutes
Total Time: 20 minutes
Servings: 2

Directions

- Set Air Fryer to 360° and preheat for 3 minutes.
- Toss the fries with olive oil until evenly coated. Season with salt and pepper.
- Pull out the basket and basket holder and add fries. Close the Air Fryer and set the timer to 15 minutes. Shake the basket every 5 minutes to help the fries cook evenly.
- Cook for an additional 3-5 minutes if the fries are still gold and shiny. The fries are ready when they are a rich golden brown.
- Season with more salt and pepper and top with chopped parsley.

Air-Fryer Empanadas

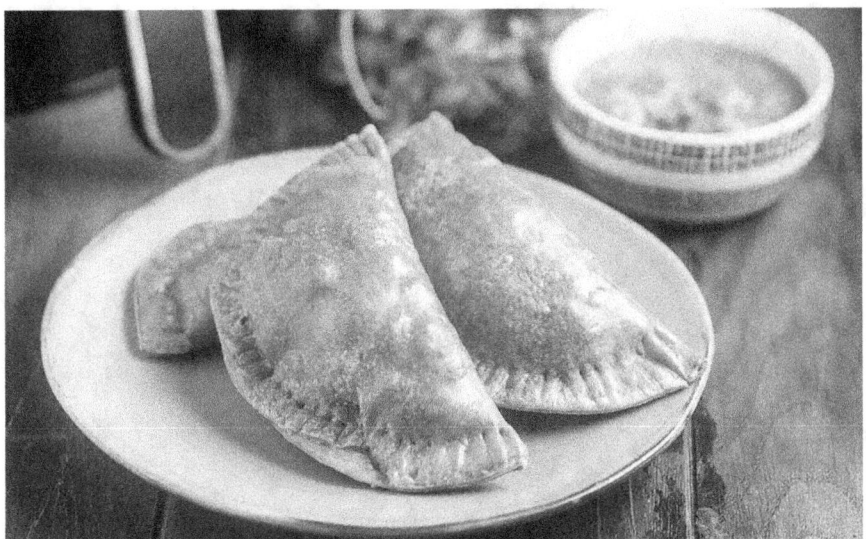

Ingredients

- 1-2 Tablespoons Of Olive Oil
- 2 Pounds Of Lean Ground Beef
- 1/2 Onion Chopped
- 2 Cloves Garlic Minced
- 1/2 Tablespoon Of Adobo Seasoning
- 2 Teaspoons Of Dried Oregano
- 1 Packet Of Sazon Optional
- 2 Tablespoons Of Cilantro Chopped
- 1/4 Cup Of Shredded Cheese
- 15 Dough Discs
- 15 Slices Of Yellow Cheese

Course:
Cuisine: American
Prep Time: 20 minutes
Cook Time:18 minutes
Total Time: 38 minutes
Servings: 8

Directions

1. In a large pan over medium high heat, warm oil. Once oil is warmed, add beef, onions, and Adobo seasoning.
2. Brown beef, about 6-7 minutes.
3. Drain ground beef.
4. Add remaining seasonings and cilantro. Cook an additional minute. Add shredded cheese, if desired. Melt cheese.
5. To each dough disc, add a slice of cheese to the center, and add 3-4 tablespoons of meat mixture over the cheese slice.
6. Fold over the dough disc, and with a fork, crimple edges and set to the side.
7. Preheat Air Fryer at 370 degrees for three minutes.
8. Once three minutes are over, spray Air Fryer pan with cooking spray and add 3-4 pastelillos to the basket. Close basket, and set to 370 degrees and cook for 7 minutes. After 7 minutes, check on it. Cook up to an additional 3 minutes, or desired level of crispness, if desired.
9. Repeat until finished.

Air-Fryer Donuts

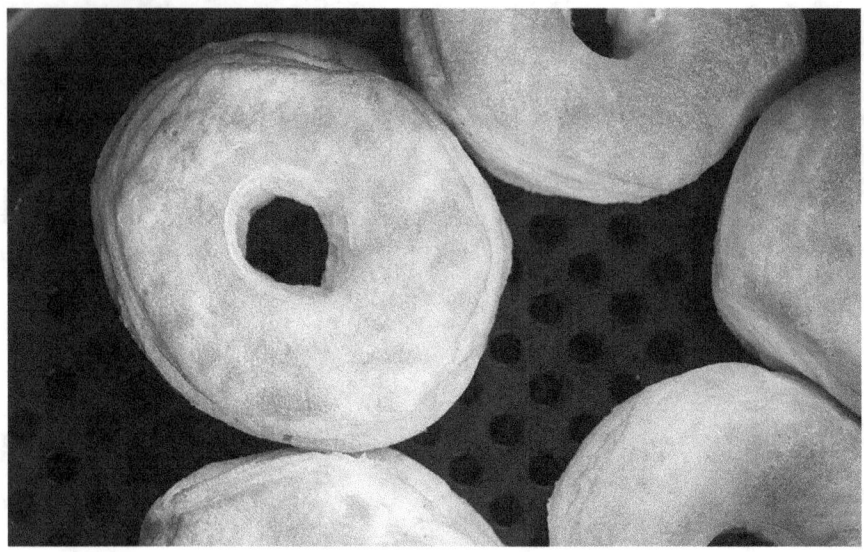

Ingredients

- 2 Cups All-Purpose Flour
- 2 Tsps Ground Cinnamon
- 1 Tsp Baking Soda
- 1 Tsp Ground Ginger
- 1/2 Tsp Ground Cloves
- 1/2 Tsp Sea Salt
- 1 Stick Butter, At Room Temperature
- 1/2 Cup Brown Sugar
- 2 Whole Eggs
- 1 Tbs Grated Lemon Zest
- 1/2 Cup Unsulphured Molasses
- 1 Cup Whole Milk
- Vegetable Oil Spray

Course:
Cuisine: American
Prep Time: 15 minutes
Cook Time: 9 minutes
Total Time: 24 minutes
Servings: 6

Directions

1. In a large bowl, combine the flour, cinnamon, baking soda, ginger, cloves, and salt.

2. Add the softened butter, sugar, eggs, lemon zest, molasses, and milk. Stir or beat with a hand mixer until everything is incorporated and smooth. Set this aside.

3. Preheat your air fryer to 320°F and set the timer for long enough to cook all the batches.

4. Spray the silicone donut molds with a little oil. Fill each with the batter. Place as many donut molds as will fit in the basket or on the crisper plate. Cook until browned and done in the center, approximately 9 minutes. Continue to cook for another minute if not the right texture.

5. Serve while warm.

Air-Fryer Apple Chips

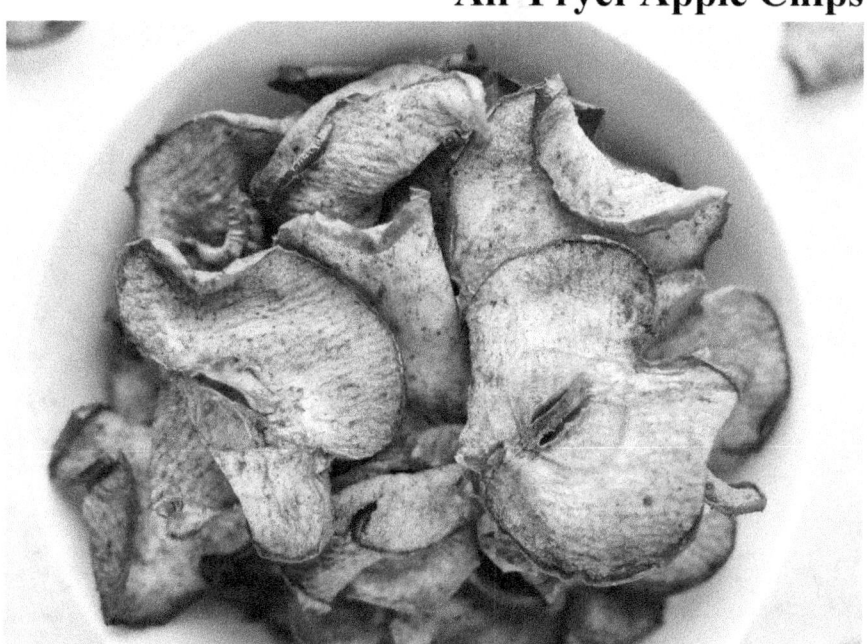

Ingredients

- 2 Apples, Thinly Sliced
- 2 Tsp. Granulated Sugar
- 1/2 Tsp. Cinnamon

Course:
Cuisine: American
Prep Time: 5 minutes
Cook Time:30 minutes
Total Time: 35 minutes
Servings: 1

Directions

FOR AIR FRYER

1. In a large bowl toss apples with cinnamon and sugar. Working in batches, place apples in a single layer in basket of air fryer (some overlap is okay).

2. Bake at 350° for about 12 minutes, flipping every 4 minutes.

FOR OVEN

1. Preheat oven to 200°. In a large bowl, toss apples with sugar and cinnamon.

2. Place a metal rack inside a rimmed baking sheet. Lay apples slices on top of rack, spacing them so that no apples overlap.

3. Bake for 2 to 3 hours, flipping apples halfway through, until apples dried out but still pliable. (Apples will continue to crisp while cooling.)

Air-Fryer Meatballs

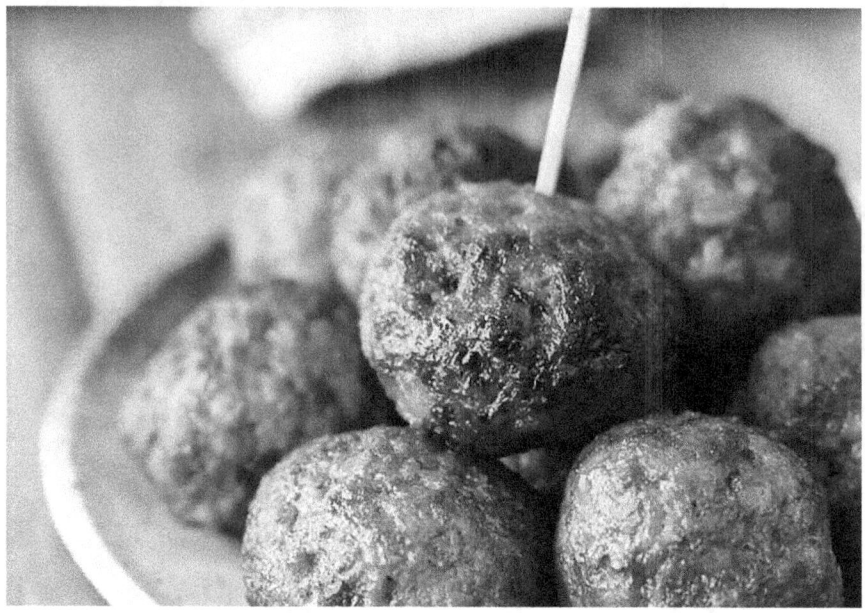

Ingredients

- 1 Pound Ground Beef
- 1 Pound Mild Italian Sausage
- ¼ Cup Onion, Minced
- 2 Cloves Garlic, Minced
- 2 Tablespoons Parsley, Chopped
- 2 Eggs
- 1½ Cup Parmesan Cheese, Grated
- Salt And Pepper
- ½ Teaspoon Crushed Red Pepper Flakes
- ½ Teaspoon Italian Seasoning
- Salt And Pepper To Taste

Course:
Cuisine: American
Prep Time: 10 minutes
Cook Time: 8 minutes
Total Time: 18 minutes
Servings: 25 Meatballs

Directions

1. Add beef, pork, onion, garlic, parsley, eggs and cheese to a large bowl.
2. Sprinkle meat mixture with a pinch of salt and pepper.
3. Mix with your hands until combined.
4. Form into 1 or 2 inch meatballs - this recipe will make about 25 meatballs.
5. Lightly spray sir fryer basket with olive oil cooking spray.
6. Add meatballs to air fryer basket, making sure they don't touch too much or over crowd the basket (work in batches if needed.)
7. Cook in air fryer for 13 minutes at 350 degrees, removing basket around 8 minutes to quickly rotate meatballs.
8. Meatballs should be 165 degrees internally when a thermometer is placed into the thickest part of the meatball.

Air-Fryer Hard Boiled Eggs

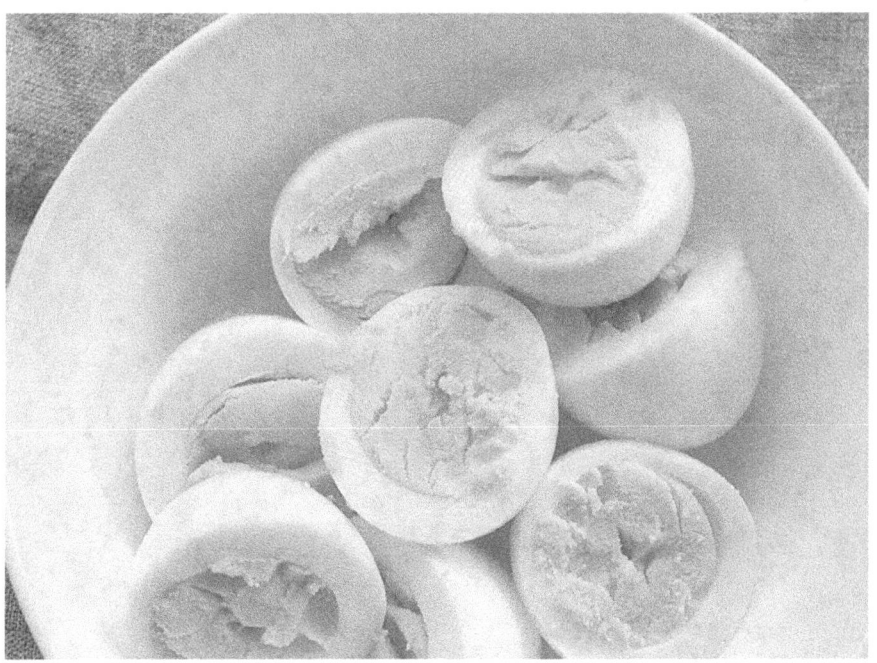

Ingredients

• 6 Large Eggs (Cold)

Course:
Cuisine: American
Prep Time: 5 minutes
Cook Time:13 minutes
Total Time: 18 minutes
Servings: 1

Directions

1. Preheat air fryer 5 minutes at 300°.
2. Add eggs to the fryer basket and cook for 13 minutes for a hard-boiled egg.
3. Remove eggs and place them in a bowl of ice water.
4. To peel, wait until eggs are cooled and shake in bowl or glass.

Notes

1. Soft boiled eggs: Cook for 9 minutes.

2. Medium boiled eggs: Cook for 11 minutes.

3. Cook time: Time may vary based on the make and model of your air fryer. Test one egg prior to cooking whole patch to ensure desired texture of yolk.

4. Trick for peeling: Place egg in about 1/2 full glass of water. Place hand or cover over the opening and shake violently until egg shell begins to crack.

Air-Fryer Beefy Swiss Bundles

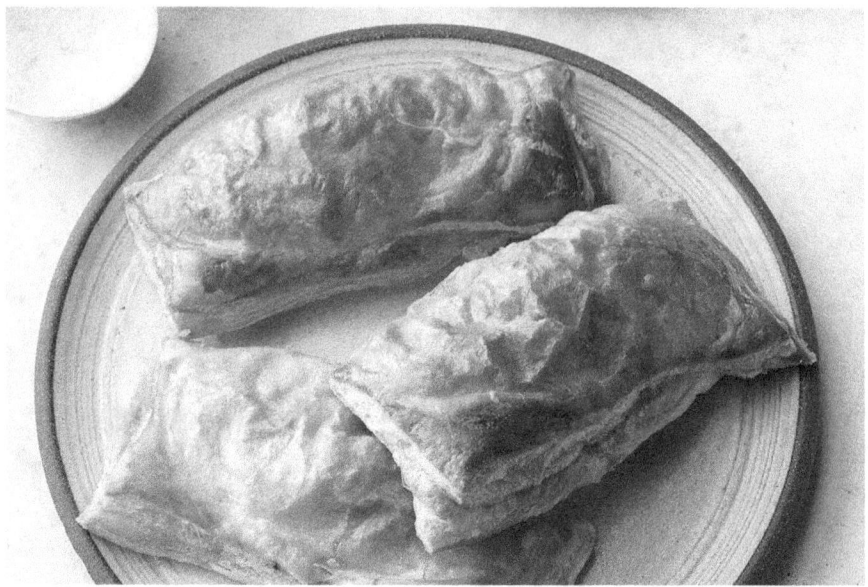

Ingredients

- 1 Pound Ground Beef
- 1-1/2 Cups Sliced Fresh Mushrooms
- 1/2 Cup Chopped Onion
- 1-1/2 Teaspoons Minced Garlic
- 4 Teaspoons Worcestershire Sauce
- 3/4 Teaspoon Dried Rosemary, Crushed
- 3/4 Teaspoon Paprika
- 1/2 Teaspoon Salt
- 1/4 Teaspoon Pepper

- 1 Sheet Frozen Puff Pastry, Thawed
- 2/3 Cup Refrigerated Mashed Potatoes
- 1 Cup Shredded Swiss Cheese
- 1 Large Egg
- 2 Tablespoons Water

Course:
Cuisine: American
Prep Time: 20 minutes
Cook Time:20 minutes
Total Time: 40 minutes
Servings: 4

Directions

1. In a large skillet, cook the beef, mushrooms and onion over medium heat until meat is no longer pink. Add garlic; cook 1 minute longer. Drain. Stir in Worcestershire sauce and seasonings. Remove from the heat; set aside.

2. On a lightly floured surface, roll puff pastry into a 15x13-in. rectangle. Cut into four 7-1/2x6-1/2-in. rectangles. Place about 2 tablespoons potatoes over each rectangle; spread to within 1 in. of edges. Top each with 3/4 cup beef mixture; sprinkle with 1/4 cup cheese.

3. Beat egg and water; brush some over pastry edges. Bring opposite corners of pastry over each bundle; pinch seams to seal. Transfer to a greased baking sheet; brush with remaining egg mixture. Bake at 400° for 17-20 minutes or until golden brown.

6. Freeze option: Freeze unbaked pastries on a waxed paper-lined baking sheet until firm. Transfer to an airtight container; return to freezer. To use, bake pastries on a parchment-lined baking sheet in a preheated 400° oven 20-25 minutes or until golden brown and heated through.
air fryer Whole Eggs recipe

Air-Fryer Ground Beef Wellington

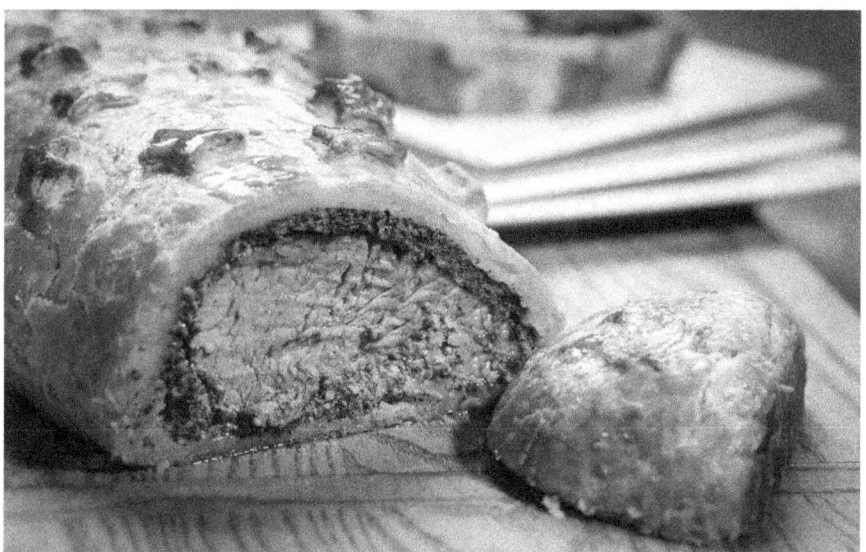

Ingredients

- 1/2 Cup Chopped Fresh Mushrooms
- 1 Tablespoon Butter
- 2 Teaspoons All-Purpose Flour
- 1/4 Teaspoon Pepper, Divided
- 1/2 Cup Half-And-Half Cream
- 1 Large Egg Yolk
- 2 Tablespoons Finely Chopped Onion
- 1/4 Teaspoon Salt
- 1/2 Pound Ground Beef
- 1 Tube (4 Ounces) Refrigerated Crescent Rolls
- Large Egg, Lightly Beaten, Optional
- 1 Teaspoon Dried Parsley Flakes

Course:
Cuisine: American
Prep Time: 30 minutes
Cook Time: 25 minutes
Total Time: 55 minutes
Servings: 2

Directions

1. In a saucepan, saute mushrooms in butter until softened. Stir in flour and 1/8 teaspoon pepper until blended. Gradually add the cream. Bring to a boil; cook and stir until thickened, about 2 minutes. Remove from the heat and set aside.

2. In a bowl, combine the egg yolk, onion, 2 tablespoons mushroom sauce, salt and remaining 1/8 teaspoon pepper. Crumble beef over mixture and mix well. Shape into 2 loaves. Separate crescent dough into 2 rectangles on a baking sheet. Seal perforations. Place a meat loaf on each rectangle. Bring dough edges together and pinch to seal. If desired, brush with egg wash. Bake at 350° until golden brown and a thermometer inserted into meat loaf reads 160°, 24-28 minutes.

3. Meanwhile, warm remaining sauce over low heat; stir in parsley. Serve sauce with Wellingtons.

Air-Fryer Cinnamon Bacon

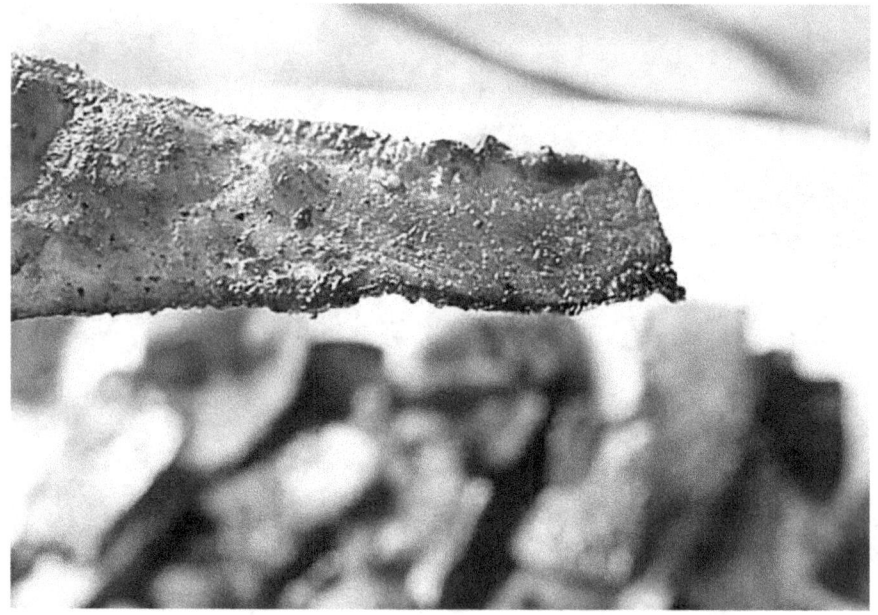

Ingredient

- ½ Cup Finely Crushed Buttery Crackers
- ½ Teaspoon Garlic Powder
- ½ Teaspoon Seafood Seasoning
- 2 Tablespoons Butter, Melted
- 1 Pound Sea Scallops, Patted Dry
- Cooking Spray

Course:
Cuisine: American
Prep Time: 5 minutes
Cook Time:15 minutes
Total Time: 20 minutes
Servings: 7 slices

Directions

Step 1 - Preheat the air fryer to 390 degrees F (198 degrees C).

Step 2 - Mix cracker crumbs, garlic powder, and seafood seasoning together in a shallow bowl. Place melted butter in a second shallow bowl.

Step 3 - Dip each scallop in the melted butter and then roll in the breading until completely coated. Set on a plate and repeat with the remaining scallops.

Step 4 - Lightly spray the air fryer basket with cooking spray. Arrange scallops in the prepared basket so that they are not touching each other; you may need to work in batches.

Step 5 - Cook in the preheated air fryer for 2 minutes. Turn scallops over gently with a small spatula and cook until opaque, about 2 more minutes.

Air-Fryer Turkey Croquettes

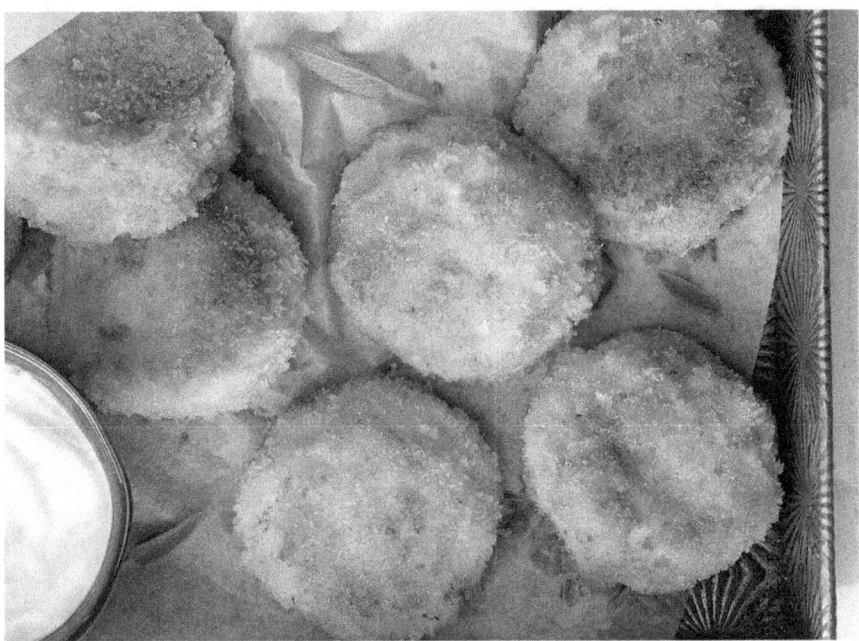

Ingredients

- 2 Cups Mashed Potatoes
  (With Added Milk And Butter)
- 1/2 Cup Grated Parmesan Cheese
- 1/2 Cup Shredded Swiss Cheese
- 1 Shallot, Finely Chopped
- 2 Teaspoons Minced Fresh Rosemary Or
  1/2 Teaspoon Dried Rosemary, Crushed
- 1 Teaspoon Minced Fresh Sage
  Or 1/4 Teaspoon Dried Sage Leaves
- 1/2 Teaspoon Salt
- 1/4 Teaspoon Pepper
- 3 Cups Finely Chopped Cooked Turkey

Course:
Cuisine: American
Prep Time: 20 minutes
Cook Time: 10 minutes
Total Time: 30 minutes
Servings: 6

- 1 Large Egg
- 2 Tablespoons Water
- 1-1/4 Cups Panko Bread Crumbs
- Butter-Flavored Cooking Spray
- Sour Cream, Optional

Directions

• In a large bowl, combine mashed potatoes, cheeses, shallot, rosemary, sage, salt and pepper; stir in turkey. Shape into twelve 1-in.-thick patties.

• In a shallow bowl, whisk egg and water. Place bread crumbs in another shallow bowl. Dip croquettes in egg mixture, then in bread crumbs, patting to help coating adhere.

• In batches, place croquettes in a single layer on greased tray in air-fryer basket; spritz with cooking spray. Cook until golden brown, 4-5 minutes. Turn; spritz with cooking spray. Cook until golden brown; 4-5 minutes. If desired, serve with sour cream.

Air-Fryer Easiest Cinnamon Roll

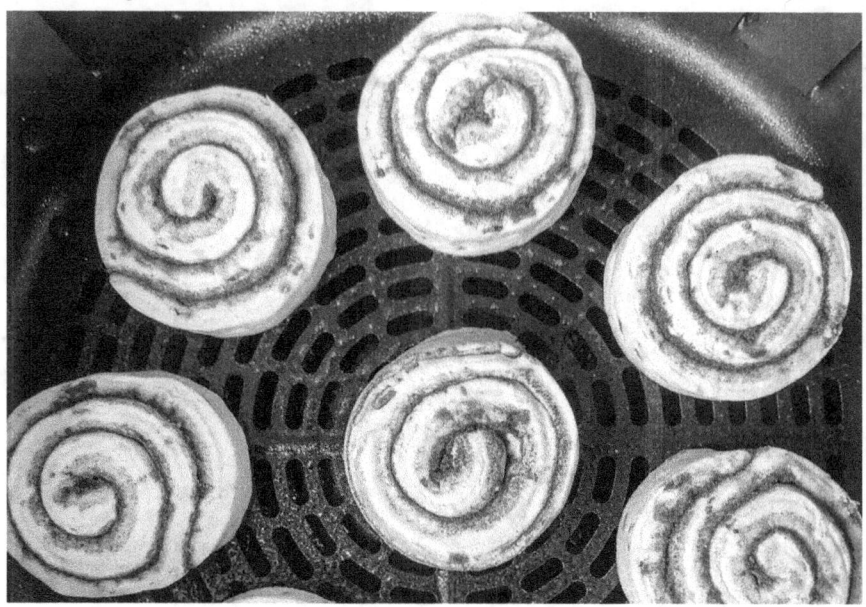

Ingredients

- 1 Pie Crust (Roll, Sold In The Dairy Department)
- 2 Tablespoons Melted Butter
- 1/4 Cup Sugar
- 2 Teaspoon Gorund Cinnamon

Icing:

- 1 Cup Powdered Sugar
- 2–3 Tablespoons Milk

Course:
Cuisine: American
Prep Time: 10 minutes
Cook Time:10 minutes
Total Time: 20 minutes
Servings: 15 cookies

Directions

1. Start by laying the pie dough on a flat surface.
2. Use your pizza cutter to make a square. (trim the excess pie dough)
3. In one bowl, add some melted butter.
4. In another bowl, mix together the sugar and ground cinnamon.
5. Use a pastry brush and rub the melted butter on top. Then sprinkle the cinnamon and sugar mixture on top of the butter.
6. Then roll up the dough.
7. Use a sharp knife and cut the pieces about 1/2 inch thick.
8. Place the cookies on the air fryer tray or in the air fryer basket (if you use a basket, you need to line in with parchment paper)
9. Set the temperature to 320 degrees F, for 6-9 minutes. The exact time will depend on your air fryer.
10. While the cookies are air frying, make the icing. Then let the cookies slightly cool, and then drizzle the icing on top, and sprinkle some of the cinnamon/sugar mixture on top.

Air-Fryer Fajita-Stuffed Chicken

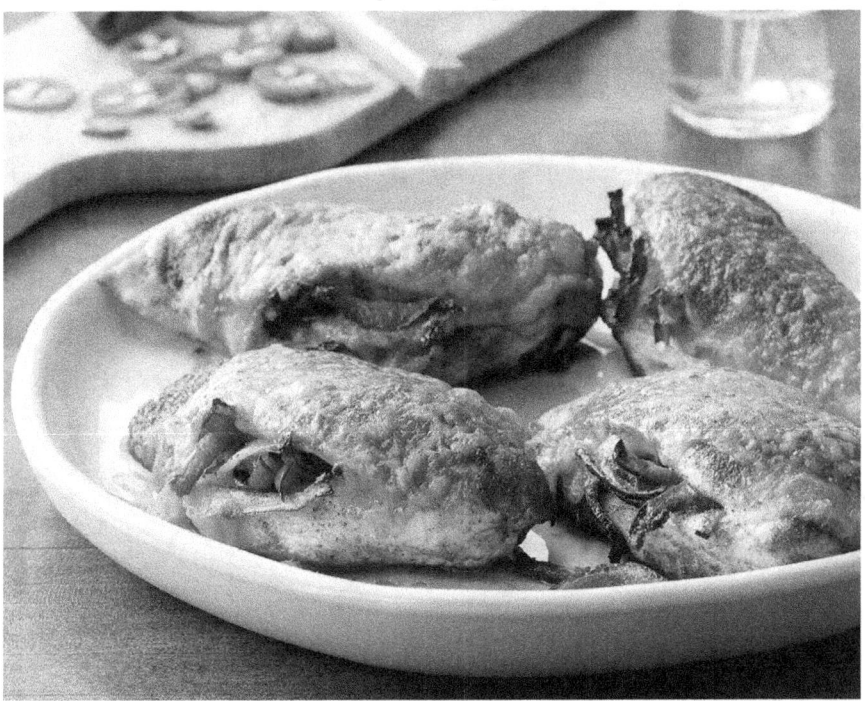

Ingredients

- 4 Boneless Skinless Chicken Breast Halves (6 Ounces Each)
- 1 Small Onion, Halved And Thinly Sliced
- 1/2 Medium Green Pepper, Thinly Sliced
- 1 Tablespoon Olive Oil
- 1 Tablespoon Chili Powder
- 1 Teaspoon Ground Cumin
- 1/2 Teaspoon Salt
- 1/4 Teaspoon Garlic Powder
- 4 Ounces Cheddar Cheese, Cut Into 4 Slices
- Optional: Salsa, Sour Cream, Minced Fresh Cilantro, Jalapeno Slices And Guacamole

Course:
Cuisine: American
Prep Time: 20 minutes
Cook Time:15 minutes
Total Time: 35 minutes
Servings: 4

Directions

• Cut a pocket horizontally in the thickest part of each chicken breast. Fill with onion and green pepper. In a small bowl, combine olive oil and seasonings; rub over chicken.

• In batches, place chicken on greased tray in air-fryer basket. Cook 6 minutes. Top chicken with cheese slices; secure with toothpicks. Cook until a thermometer inserted in chicken reads at least 165°, 6-8 minutes longer. Discard toothpicks. If desired, serve with toppings of your choice.

Air-Fryer Spanakopita Bites

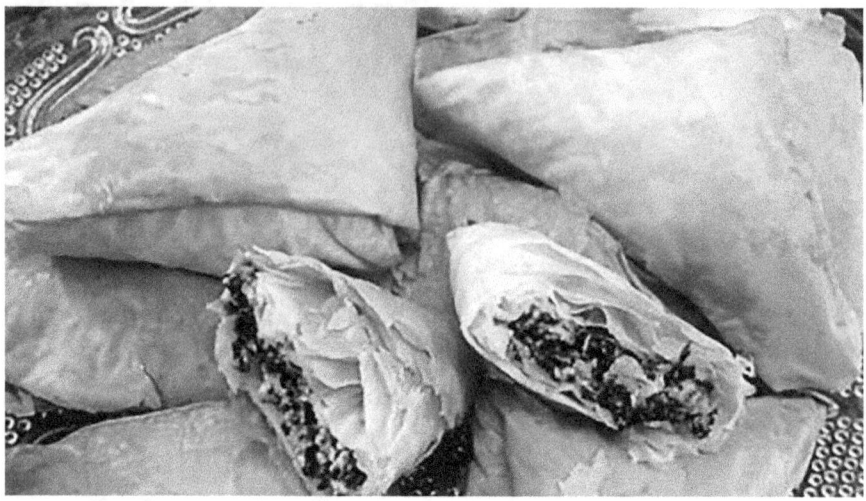

Ingredients

- 1⁄2 Cup Vegetable Oil
- 2 Large Onions, Chopped
- 2 (10 Ounce) Packages Frozen Chopped Spinach, Thawed, Drained And Squeezed Dry
- 2 Tablespoons Chopped Fresh Dill
- 2 Tablespoons All-Purpose Flour
- 2 (4 Ounce) Packages Feta Cheese, Crumbled
- 4 Eggs, Lightly Beaten
- Salt And Pepper
- 1 (24 Ounce) Package Phyllo Dough
- 3⁄4 Lb Butter, Melted

Course:
Cuisine: American
Prep Time: 30 minutes
Cook Time:45 minutes
Total Time: 1 hr, 15 min
Servings: 27 Spanakopitas

Directions

- Preheat oven to 350 degrees F (175 degrees C).
- Heat vegetable oil in a large saucepan over medium heat.
- Slowly cook and stir onions until softened.
- Mix in spinach, dill and flour.
- Cook approximately 10 minutes, or until most of the moisture has been absorbed.
- Remove from heat.
- Mix in feta cheese, eggs, salt and pepper.
- Lay phyllo dough flat and brush with butter.
- Place a small amount of spinach mixture onto each piece of dough.
- Fold phyllo into triangles around the mixture.
- Brush with butter.
- Place filled phyllo dough triangles on a large baking sheet.
- Bake in the preheated oven 45 minutes to 1 hour, or until golden brown.

Air-Fryer Sweet Potato Fries

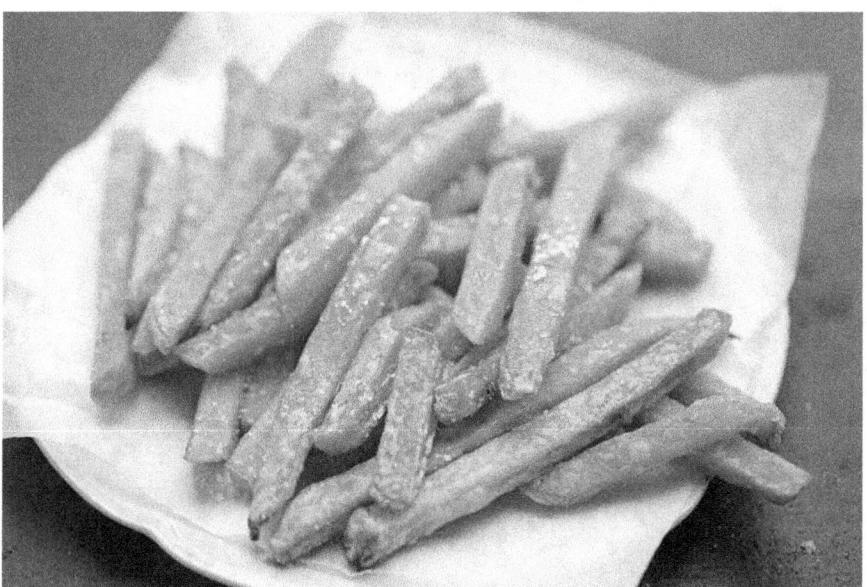

Ingredients

- 16 Ounces Sweet Potato
  (I Used One Large, Weighed On My Food Scale
  Between 14 - 16 Ounces Works)
- 1/2 Teaspoon Course Sea Salt (Or More, To Taste)
- 1/4 Teaspoon Black Pepper
- 1/4 Teaspoon Paprika
- 2 Teaspoons Avocado Oil (Or Oil Of Choice)

Course: Side Dish
Cuisine: American
Prep Time: 4 minutes
Cook Time:20 minutes
Total Time: 24 minutes
Servings: 2 servings

Directions

1. Preheat your air fryer to 380 degrees.
2. Slice up your sweet potato into pinkie finger sized sticks (mine are between 1/4 and 1/2 inch).
3. I don't measure, and they don't have to be perfect, but try to keep the size fairly consistent.
3. Place the potato slices in a mixing bowl, along with the oil, salt, pepper and paprika, and toss to coat.
4. Transfer fry mixture to the air fryer, and cook until tender and crispy (about 20 minutes).
5. Shake the basket a few times to rearrange the fries, and use a flipper to flip them.
6. Use your own judgement, cooking longer or shorter, if needed, keeping an eye on the fries to make sure they don't burn.
7. Taste test, and add more salt if needed.

Crispy Air-Fried Onion Rings

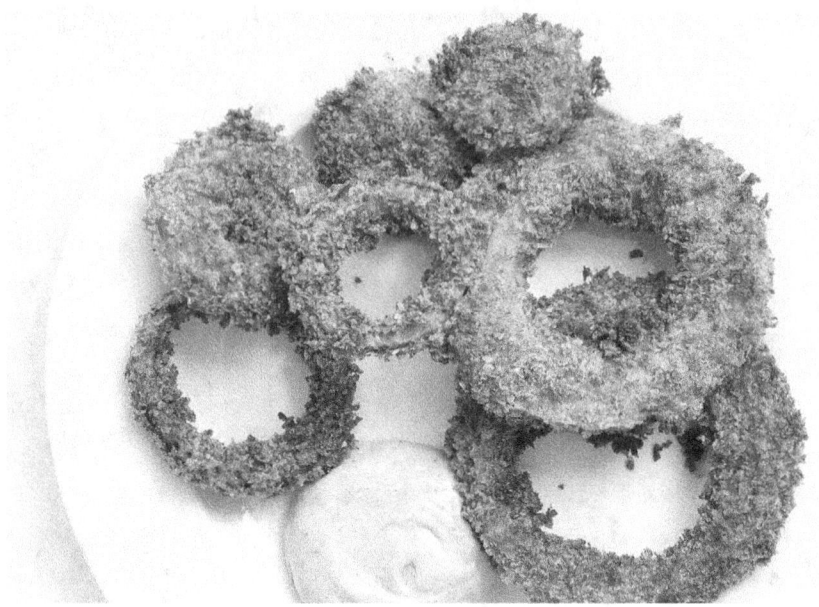

Ingredients

- 2 Large Sweet Onions
- 3/4 Cup All-Purpose Flour
- 2 Eggs
- 2 Tablespoons Milk
- 2 Cups Panko Breadcrumbs
- 1 Teaspoon Smoked Paprika
- 1/2 Teaspoon Onion Powder
- 1/2 Teaspoon Garlic Powder
- 2 Teaspoons Salt
- Optional: Creamy Dipping Sauces, Honey Mustard, Or Ketchup (For Serving)

Course:
Cuisine: American
Prep Time: 15 minutes
Cook Time:11 minutes
Total Time: 26 minutes
Servings: 18 Onion rings

Directions

1. Cut off both ends of the onions and peel off the skin.
2. Peeled raw onion on a cutting board
3. Slice the onions into thick rings.
4. Sliced onions on a cutting board
5. Carefully separate the rings from each other. Set aside the innermost rings for another recipe. If the rings break, you can still use them.
6. Raw onion rings: Prepare the 3 dredging bowls. Put the flour in 1 shallow bowl. Beat the eggs and milk in another shallow bowl. Add the panko breadcrumbs to a third shallow bowl. In a separate small bowl, mix the smoked paprika, onion powder, garlic powder, and salt, then divide the mixture evenly among each of the bowls. Whisk each bowl to disperse the seasonings.
7. Breadcrumbs, flour, and egg wash in bowls

Air-Fried Corn Dog Bites

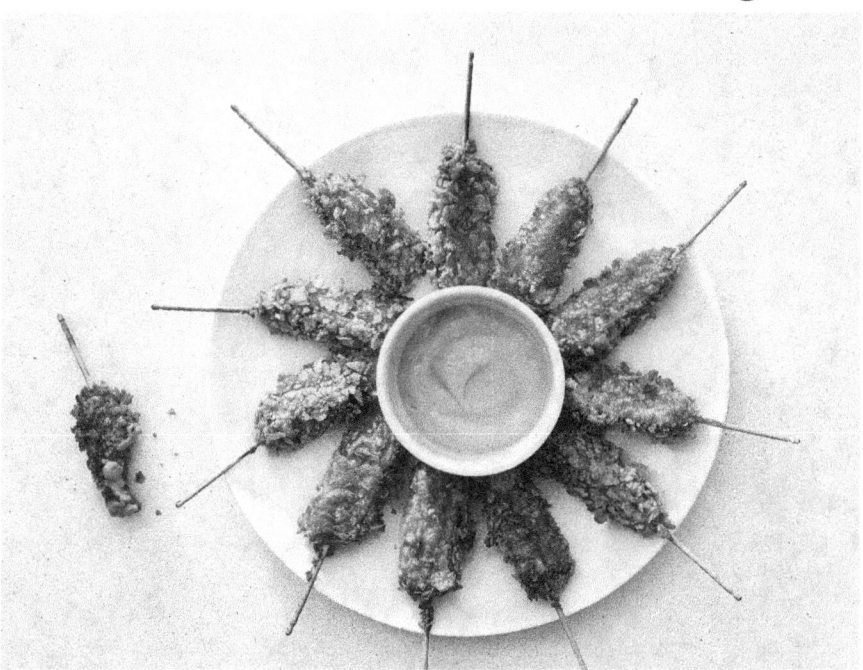

Ingredients

- 2 Uncured All-Beef Hot Dogs
- 12 Craft Sticks Or Bamboo Skewers
- 1/2 Cup (About 2 1/8 Oz.) All-Purpose Flour
- 2 Large Eggs, Lightly Beaten
- 1 1/2 Cups Finely Crushed Cornflakes Cereal
- Cooking Spray
- 8 Teaspoons Yellow Mustard

Course:
Cuisine: American
Prep Time: 20 minutes
Cook Time: 15 minutes
Total Time: 35 minutes
Servings: 4

Directions

Step 1 - Slice each hot dog in half lengthwise. Cut each half into 3 equal pieces. Insert a craft stick or bamboo skewer into 1 end of each piece of hot dog.

Step 2 - Place flour in a shallow dish. Place lightly beaten eggs in a second shallow dish. Place crushed cornflakes in a third shallow dish. Dredge hot dogs in flour, shaking off excess. Dip in egg, allowing any excess to drip off. Dredge in cornflake crumbs, pressing to adhere.

Step 3 - Lightly coat air fryer basket with cooking spray. Place 6 corn dog bites in basket; lightly spray tops with cooking spray. Cook at 375°F until coating is golden brown and crunchy, 10 minutes, turning the corn dog bites over halfway through cooking. Repeat with remaining corn dog bites.

Step 4 - To serve, place 3 corn dog bites on each plate with 2 teaspoons mustard, and serve immediately.

Air-Fryer Grilled Cheese Sandwich

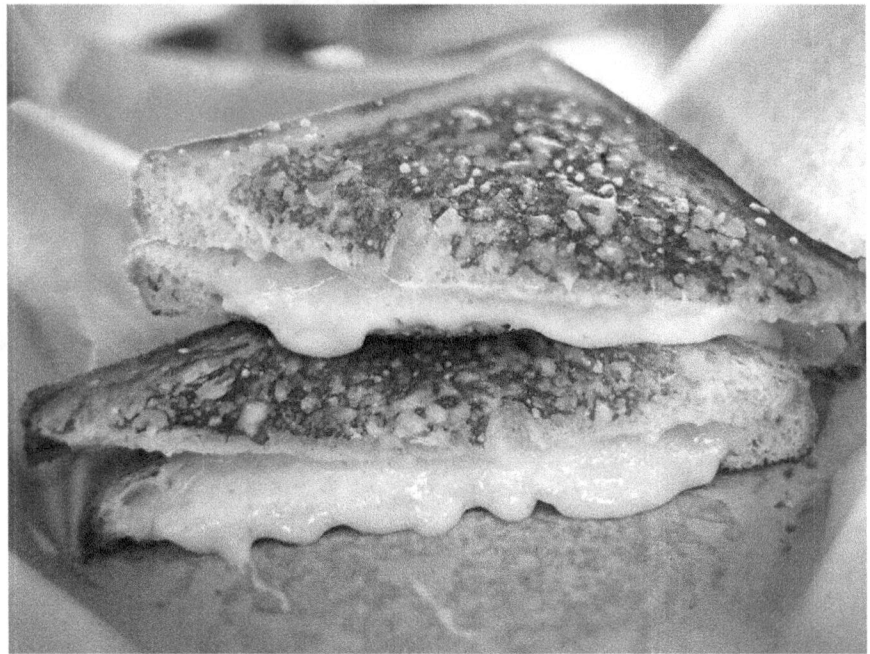

Ingredients

- 1 Piece American Cheese
- 2 Pieces Bread
- 1 Can Olive Oil Cooking Spray

Course:
Cuisine: American
Prep Time: 2 minutes
Cook Time: 4 minutes
Total Time: 8 minutes
Servings:

Directions

1. Preheat air fryer or oven to 400 degrees.
2. Spray one side of each piece of bread with the olive oil cooking spray.
3. Place the American cheese between the bread, olive oil sprayed side facing out.
4. Cook in the air fryer or oven for 4 minutes on the lowest shelf, flipping exactly halfway through.
5. After the cook time is over, allow the sandwich to rest in the warm air fryer or oven for 2 or 3 minutes to allow for the cheese to melt.

Air-Fryer Veggie Quesadillas

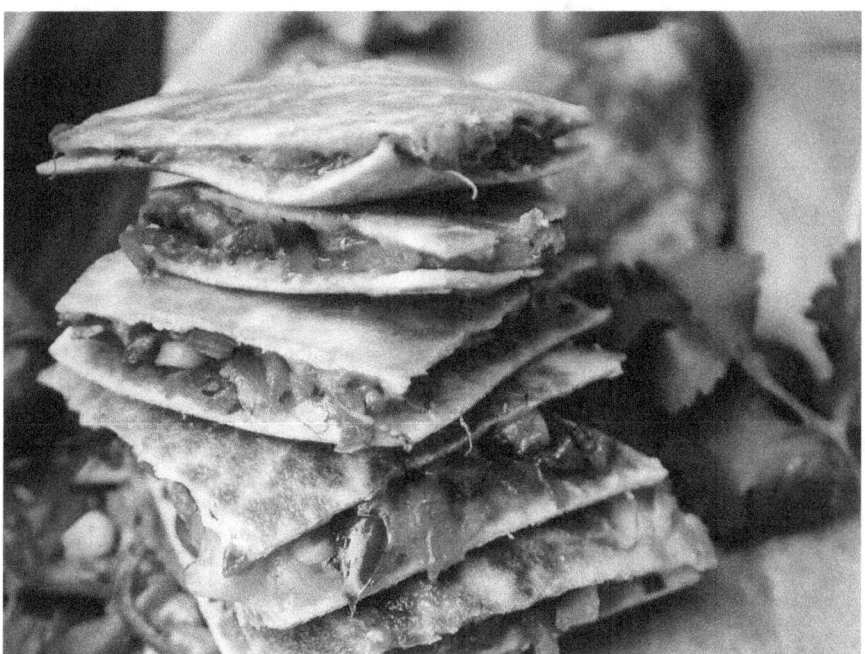

Ingredients

Course:
Cuisine: American
Prep Time: 10 minutes
Cook Time:15 minutes
Restimg Time: 2 minutes
Total Time: 27 minutes
Servings: 6

- 4 (6-In.) Sprouted Whole-Grain Flour Tortillas
- 4 Oz Reduced-Fat Sharp Cheddar Cheese, Shredded (About 1 Cup)
- 1 Cup Sliced Red Bell Pepper
- 1 Cup Sliced Zucchini
- 1 Cup No-Salt-Added Canned Black Beans, Drained And Rinsed
- Cooking Spray
- 2 Oz Plain 2% Reduced-Fat Greek Yogurt
- 1 Tsp Lime Zest Plus
- 1 Tbsp. Fresh Juice (From 1 Lime)
- ¼ Tsp Ground Cumin
- 2 Tbsp Chopped Fresh Cilantro
- ½ Cup Drained Refrigerated Pico De Gallo

Directions

Place tortillas on a work surface. Sprinkle 2 tablespoons shredded cheese over half of each tortilla. Top cheese on each tortilla with 1/4 cup each red pepper slices, zucchini slices, and black beans. Sprinkle evenly with remaining 1/2 cup cheese. Fold tortillas over to form half-moon shaped quesadillas. Lightly coat quesadillas with cooking spray, and secure with toothpicks.

Lightly spray air fryer basket with cooking spray. Carefully place 2 quesadillas in the basket, and cook at 400°F until tortillas are golden brown and slightly crispy, cheese is melted, and vegetables are slightly softened, 10 minutes, turning quesadillas over halfway through cooking. Repeat with remaining quesadillas.

While quesadillas cook, stir together yogurt, lime zest, lime juice, and cumin in a small bowl. To serve, cut each quesadilla into wedges and sprinkle with cilantro. Serve each with 1 tablespoon cumin cream and 2 tablespoons pico de gallo.

Air-Fryer Breakfast Bombs

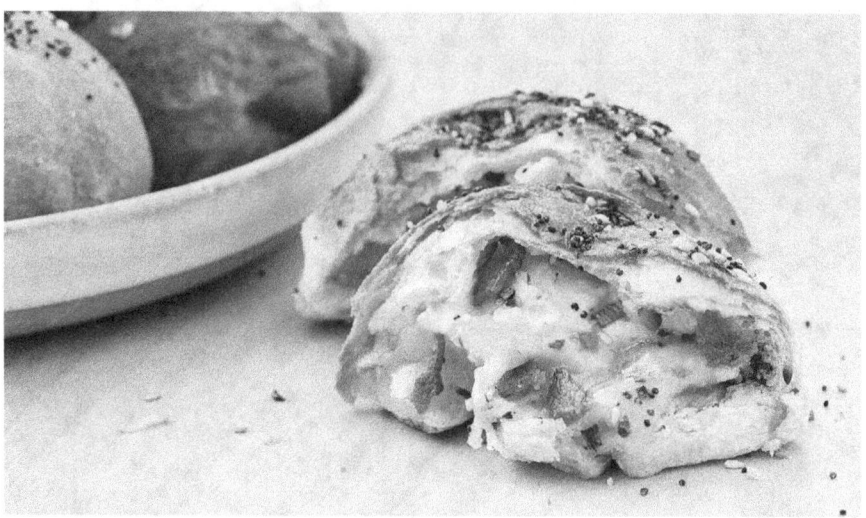

Ingredients

- 3 Center-Cut Bacon Slices
- 3 Large Eggs, Lightly Beaten
- 1 Ounce 1/3-Less-Fat Cream Cheese, Softened
- 1 Tablespoon Chopped Fresh Chives
- 4 Ounces Fresh Prepared Whole-Wheat Pizza Dough
- Cooking Spray

Course:
Cuisine: American
Prep Time: 10 minutes
Cook Time: 15 minutes
Total Time: 25 minutes
Servings: 2

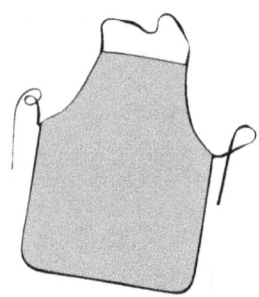

Directions

Step 1 - Cook bacon in a medium skillet over medium until very crisp, about 10 minutes. Remove bacon from pan; crumble. Add eggs to bacon drippings in pan; cook, stirring often, until almost set but still loose, about 1 minute. Transfer eggs to a bowl; stir in cream cheese, chives, and crumbled bacon.

Step 2 - Divide dough into 4 equal pieces. Roll each piece on a lightly floured surface into a 5-inch circle. Place one-fourth of egg mixture in center of each dough circle. Brush outside edge of dough with water; wrap dough around egg mixture to form a purse, pinching together dough at the seams.

Step 3 - Place dough purses in single layer in air fryer basket; coat well with cooking spray. Cook at 350°F until golden brown, 5 to 6 minutes, checking after 4 minutes.

Air-Fryer Potato Chips

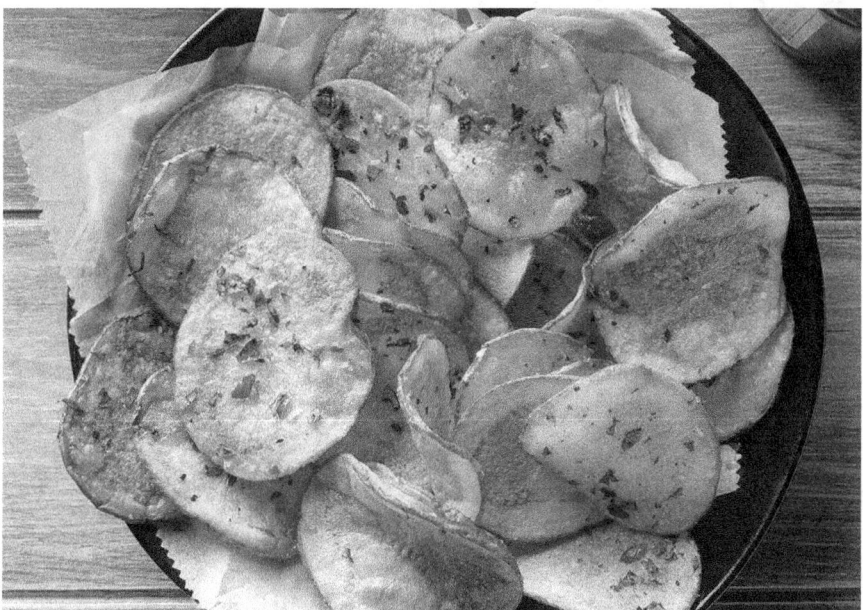

Ingredients

- 2 Yukon Gold Potatoes (About 8 Ounces Each), Scrubbed
- 1 Tablespoon Olive Oil
- Kosher Salt And Freshly Ground Black Pepper

Course:
Cuisine: American
Prep Time: 15 minutes
Cook Time: 25 minutes
Total Time: 40 minutes
Servings: 4

Directions

SPECIAL EQUIPMENT: A MANDOLINE AND A 3.5-QUART AIR FRYER

1. Thinly slice the potatoes on a mandoline, about 1/16 inch thick. Transfer to a medium bowl and run under cold water until almost all the white starch comes off and the water runs clear. Dry well between a couple paper towels. Dry the bowl as well.

2. Add the dry potatoes back to the dry bowl and toss with the oil, 1/2 teaspoon salt and a few grinds of pepper until evenly coated.

3. Preheat a 3.5-quart air fryer to 320 degrees F. Shingle the potatoes in the bottom of the basket; it's okay if there are two layers. Cook until the potatoes are deep golden brown around the edges and crisp, tossing every 5 minutes with tongs so they're evenly cooked, about 30 minutes. If you notice a few slices are finished cooking and completely crisp before others, remove to a large bowl and continue cooking the remaining pieces.

4. Season the chips with a pinch of salt. Serve immediately or let cool and store in an airtight container for up to 2 days.

Air-Fried Shrimp Spring Rolls with Sweet Chili Sauce

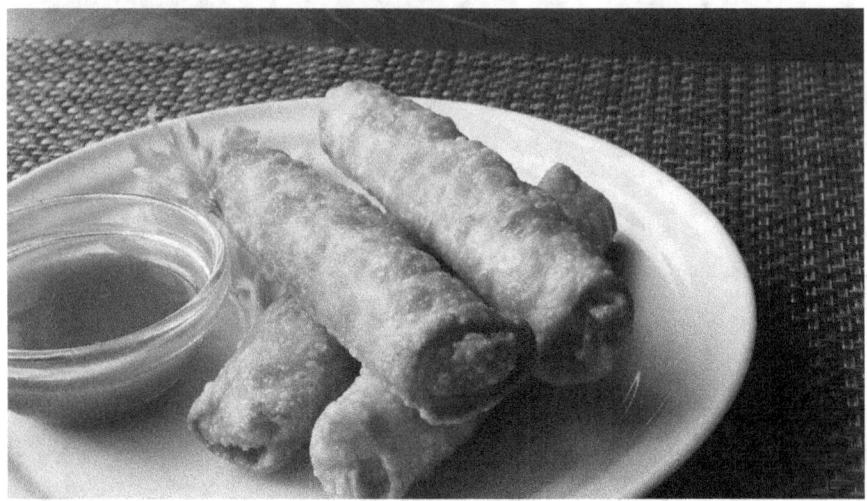

Ingredients

- 2 1/2 Tablespoons Sesame Oil, Divided
- 2 Cups Pre-Shredded Cabbage
- 1 Cup Matchstick Carrots
- 1 Cup Julienne-Cut Red Bell Pepper
- 4 Ounces Peeled,
  Deveined Raw Shrimp, Chopped
- 3/4 Cup Julienne-Cut Snow Peas
- 1/4 Cup Chopped Fresh Cilantro
- 1 Tablespoon Fresh Lime Juice

Course:
Cuisine: American
Prep Time: 15 minutes
Cook Time:20 minutes
Total Time: 35 minutes
Servings: 4

- 2 Teaspoons Fish Sauce
- 1/4 Teaspoon Crushed Red Pepper
- 8 (8-Inch-Square) Spring Roll Wrappers
- 1/2 Cup Sweet Chili Sauce

Directions

Step 1. Heat 1 1/2 teaspoons of the oil in large skillet over high until slightly smoking.

Step 2. Add cabbage, carrots, and bell pepper; cook, stirring constantly until lightly wilted, 1 to 1 1/2 minutes.

Step 3. Spread on a rimmed baking sheet; cool 5 minutes.

Step 4. Place cabbage mixture, shrimp, snow peas, cilantro, lime juice, fish sauce, and crushed red pepper in a large bowl; toss to combine.

Step 5. Place spring roll wrappers on work surface with 1 corner facing you. Spoon 1/4 cup filling in center of each spring roll wrapper, spreading from left to right into a 3-inch long strip. Fold bottom corner of each wrapper over filling, tucking tip of corner under filling. Fold left and right corners over filling. Lightly brush remaining corner with water; tightly roll filled end toward remaining corner; gently press to seal. Brush spring rolls with remaining 2 tablespoons oil.

Step 6. Place 4 spring rolls in air fryer basket, and cook at 390°F until golden, 6 to 7 minutes, turning spring rolls after 5 minutes. Repeat with remaining spring rolls. Serve with sweet chili sauce.

Air-Fryer Eggplant Parmesan

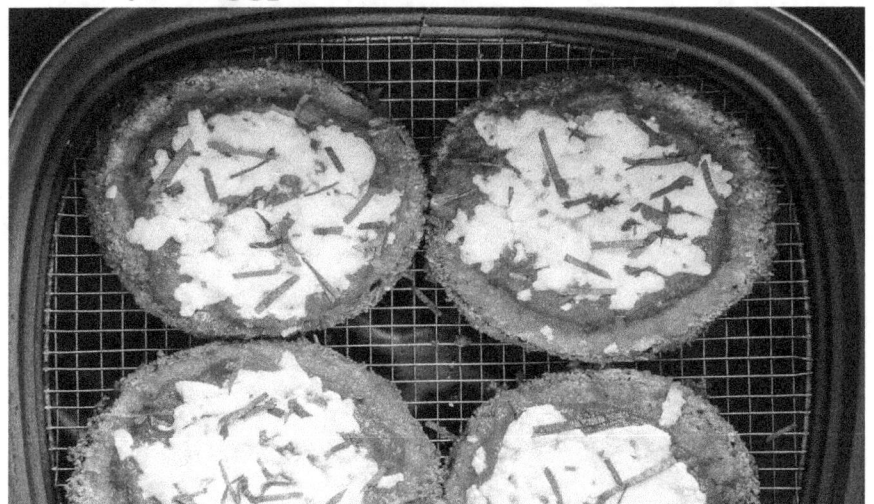

Ingredients

- 1 Medium Eggplant
- 2 Cups Italian Breadcrumbs
- 1/4 Cup Shredded Parmesan Cheese + More For Topping
- 1 Tablespoon Garlic Powder
- 1 Tablespoon Dried Parsley
- 1/2 Teaspoon Kosher Salt
- 1/4 Teaspoon Ground Black Pepper
- 2 Large Eggs
- 1 Cup Tomato Sauce
- 1 Cup Shredded Mozzarella Cheese
- Freshly Chopped Basil (Optional For Topping)

Course:
Cuisine: Italian Inspired
Prep Time: 15 minutes
Cook Time: 25 minutes
Total Time: 40 minutes
Servings: 4

Directions

1. Slice the ends off of the eggplant using a sharp knife, about 1/4 inch from the stem. Then slice the eggplant into 1/2 -inch thick rounds and place the eggplant onto a small baking sheet or plate.
2. Make the breadcrumb mixture – Combine the breadcrumbs + parmesan cheese + garlic powder + dried parsley + salt & pepper into a medium-size mixing bowl and mix to combine into a breadcrumb mixture.
3. Setup a dredging station: crack the eggs into a medium size bowl, season with salt & pepper and whisk well to combine. Then setup the breadcrumb mixture + the egg mixture+the sliced eggplant next to each other and dredge each piece of eggplant in the egg, then the breadcrumb mixture, pressing the breadcrumbs into the eggplant as you dredge them. Then place the breaded eggplant slices back onto the baking sheet. Continue until you have breaded all of the eggplant.
4. Once the air-fryer is preheated, spray the basket with olive oil cooking spray and place the eggplant pieces into the air-fryer, spray each with cooking spray. Close the basket and cook for 8 minutes, flipping each piece over and spraying the other side with cooking spray halfway through the cooking time.
5. Once they are done and super crispy, top each with some of the tomato sauce, then some shredded mozzarella cheese. Close the air-fryer and cook for 2-3 more minutes to melt the cheese.
6. Remove, top with freshly chopped basil and enjoy.

Air-Fryer Curly Zucchini Fries

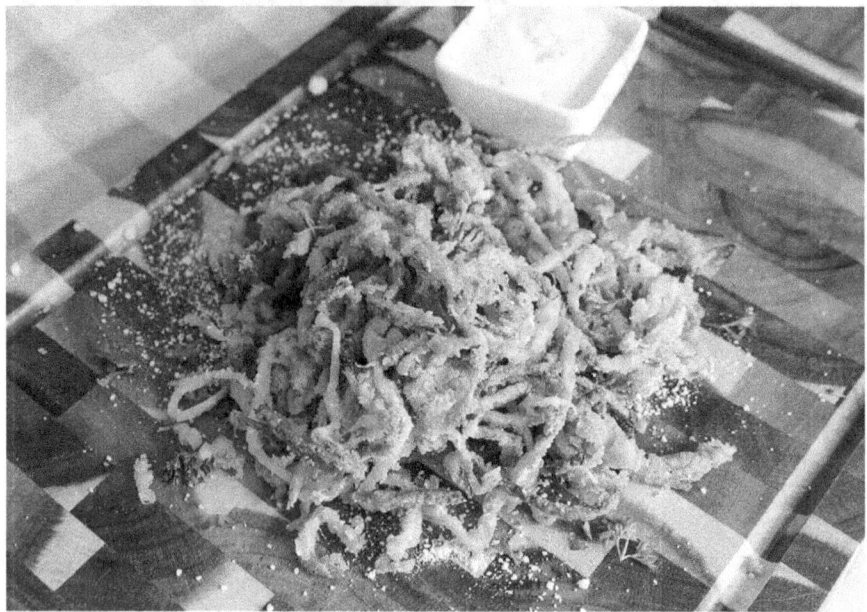

Ingredients

- 2 Medium Zucchini
- 1 Large Egg Beaten
- ½ Cup Almond Flour Or Panko/Italian Breadcrumbs
- ½ Cup Parmesan Cheese Grated
- 1 Teaspoon Italian Seasoning Or Seasoning Of Choice
- ½ Teaspoon Garlic Powder Optional
- Pinch Of Salt And Pepper
- Oil For Spraying Olive Or Oil Of Choice

Course: Appetizer
Cuisine: American
Prep Time: 5 minutes
Cook Time: 10 minutes
Total Time: 15 minutes
Servings: 4 people

Directions

1. Cut the zucchini in half and into sticks (aka fries) about 1/2 inch thick and 3-4 inches long.
2. In a shallow bowl, combine the almond flour (or bread crumbs), grated parmesan, spices and a pinch of salt and pepper. Mix to combine.
3. Dredge zucchini in egg and then in the almond flour mixture and place on a plate or baking sheet. Generously spray zucchini with cooking spray.
4. Working in batches, place the zucchini fries in a single layer in the air fryer. and Cook for 10 minutes at 400F, or until crispy.

Air-Fryer Potstickers

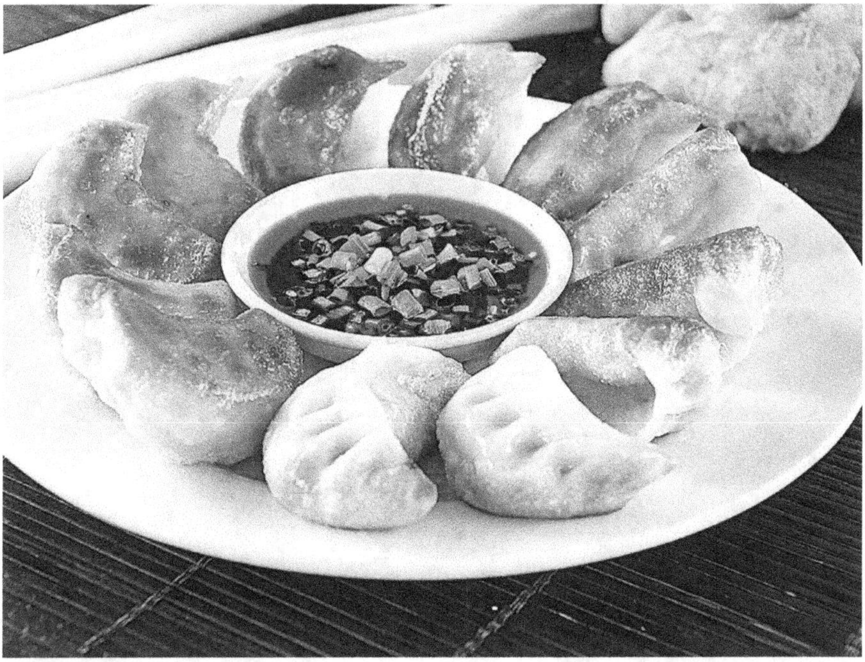

Ingredients

- ½ Pound Ground Pork
- 1 (4 Ounce) Can Water Chestnuts, Drained And Chopped
- 1 (4 Ounce) Can Shiitake Mushrooms, Drained And Chopped
- 2 Tablespoons Soy Sauce
- 2 Tablespoons Sesame Oil
- 1 Tablespoon Sriracha Sauce
- 1 (12 Ounce) Package Round Dumpling Wrappers

Course:
Cuisine: Asian
Prep Time: 10 minutes
Cook Time: 25 minutes
Total Time: 35 minutes
Servings: 24

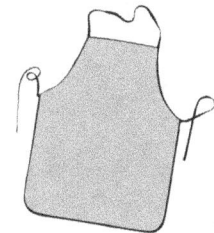

Directions

Step 1 - Preheat an air fryer to 400 degrees F (200 degrees C).

Step 2 - Combine ground pork, water chestnuts, shiitake mushrooms, sesame oil, soy sauce, and Sriracha in a large skillet over medium-high heat. Cook until pork is no longer pink, about 6 minutes. Remove from heat and let sit until cool enough to handle.

Step 3 - Lay out 8 dumpling wrappers on a clean work surface. Place a heaping teaspoonful of pork mixture in the middle of each wrapper. Pull both sides up like a taco and pinch the tops until sealed.

Step 4 - Cook in batches in the pre-heated air fryer for 3 minutes. Use tongs to flip the potstickers and cook 3 minutes more. Transfer to a paper-towel lined plate. Repeat with remaining dumpling wrappers and filling.

Air-Fryer Vegetarian Egg Rolls

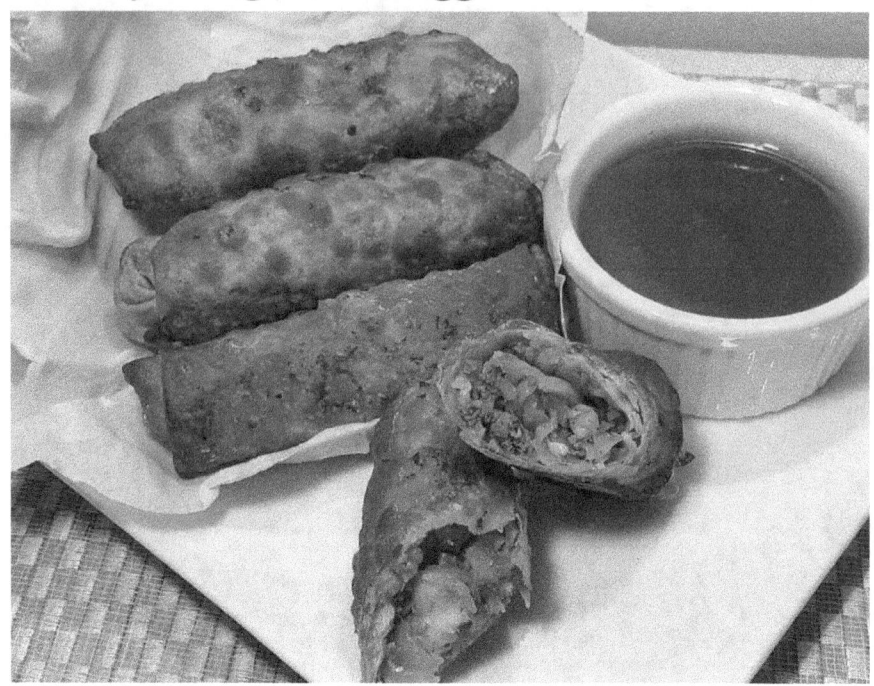

Ingredients

- 1 Tablespoon Olive Oil
- 1 Pound Ground Pork Or Chicken
- 1 Clove Garlic, Minced
- 1 Tablespoon Grated Fresh Ginger
- 1 Medium Carrot, Shredded

Course:
Cuisine: Chinese
Prep Time: 20 minutes
Cook Time: 25 minutes
Total Time: 45 minutes
Servings: 12 egg rolls

Directions

1. Preheat a frying pan for a few minutes over medium heat. Add the sesame oil, ginger, garlic, cabbage, and shredded carrot. Cook down for 2-3 minutes or until the cabbage has wilted. Add the green onions, soy sauce, and black pepper. Stir and remove from heat.

2. Assemble your egg rolls (see the detailed instructions in the post). Brush olive oil over the top of the egg rolls. Alternatively, you could use a Misto to spray olive oil, but I found that caused the egg roll wrappers to bubble up more when they were cooking.

3. Brush olive oil on the basket of your air fryer. Place the egg rolls in the basket, seam side down, without letting them touch each other.

4. Bake at 360 degrees F for 7 minutes. Flip and bake for an additional 2 minutes.

Air-Fryer Chimichangas

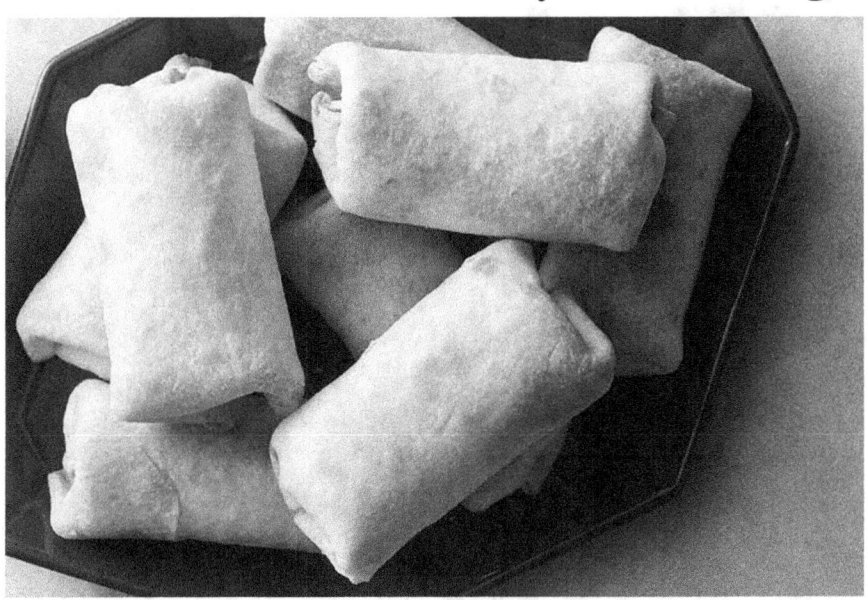

Ingredients

- 2 Teaspoon Vegetable Oil
- 2 Cups Shredded Deli Rotisserie Chicken
- 1 Packet (0.85 Oz) Chicken Taco Seasoning Mix
- 3 Tablespoons Water
- 3/4 Cup (From 16-Oz Can) Traditional Refried Beans
- 1 Can (4.5 Oz) Chopped Green Chiles
- 8 Flour Tortillas (6 Inch)
- 1 Cup Shredded Cheddar Cheese (4 Oz)
- 2 Tablespoons Butter, Melted

Course:
Cuisine: Mexican
Prep Time: 15 minutes
Cook Time:20 minutes
Total Time: 35 minutes
Servings: 8

Directions

1. In 10-inch nonstick skillet, heat oil over medium heat. Add chicken, taco seasoning mix and water; stir until well coated. Cook uncovered 4 to 5 minutes, stirring frequently, until chicken is heated through.

2. In small bowl, stir together beans and chiles. Place tortilla on work surface, and spread about 3 tablespoons of the bean mixture in middle of tortilla. Top with about 1/4 cup of the chicken and 2 tablespoons of the cheese. Fold sides of tortilla in. Fold bottom over filling and sides. Roll tightly to enclose filling. Repeat with remaining tortillas.

3. Brush outside of each filled tortilla with melted butter; place 4 in basket of air fryer, seam side down. Set to 400°F; cook 4 minutes. Turn; cook 2 to 3 minutes or until lightly browned and heated through. Repeat with remaining 4 filled tortillas.

Air-Fryer Ravioli

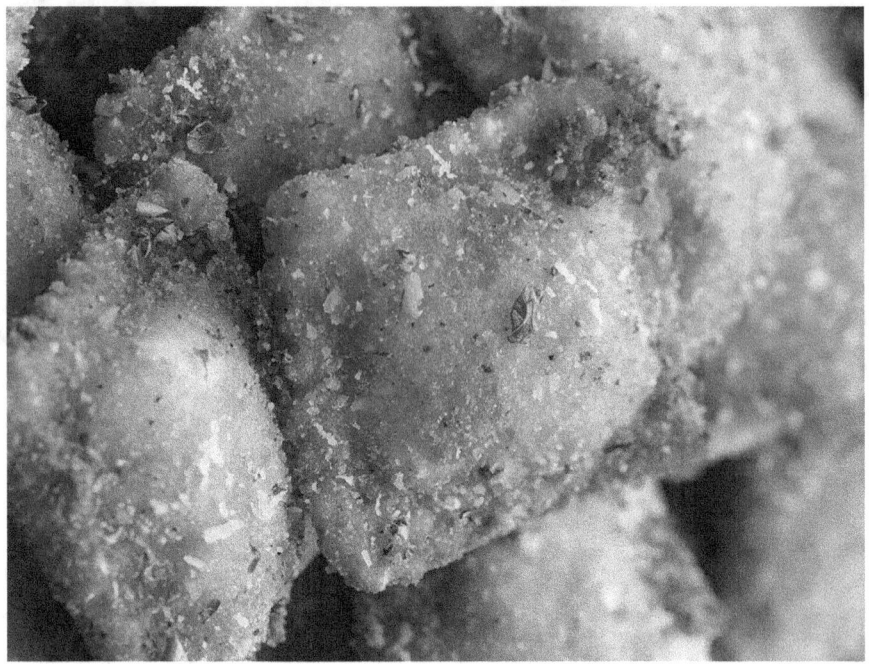

Ingredients

- Vegetable Oil
- 1 Pkg Premium Refrigerated Ravioli About 16 Pieces
- 3 Large Egg Whites
- 2 Tbsp Water
- 1 Cup Italian Seasoned Panko Breadcrumbs
- 1/2 Cup Parmesan Cheese
- 1 Cup Pizza Or Marinara Sauce

Course: Appetizer
Cuisine: Italian
Prep Time: 5 minutes
Cook Time: 5 minutes
Total Time: 10 minutes
Servings: 6

Directions

1. Lightly brush the basket of an air fryer with vegetable oil. Preheat the air fryer to 400 degrees.
2. While the air fryer is preheating, whisk together the egg whites and water in a shallow bowl.
3. Whisk the Panko breadcrumbs and Parmesan cheese together in a separate shallow bowl.
4. Dip each ravioli on both sides first in the egg and water mixture and then in the breadcrumb and cheese mixture.
5. Open the air fryer and place the coated ravioli in a single layer in the basket. You'll have to fry the ravioli in two or three batches, depending on the size of your air fryer.
6. Fry the ravioli for about 4 minutes, or until puffed and starting to brown.
7. Serve with pizza or marinara sauce for dipping.

Air-Fryer Chinese Egg Roll

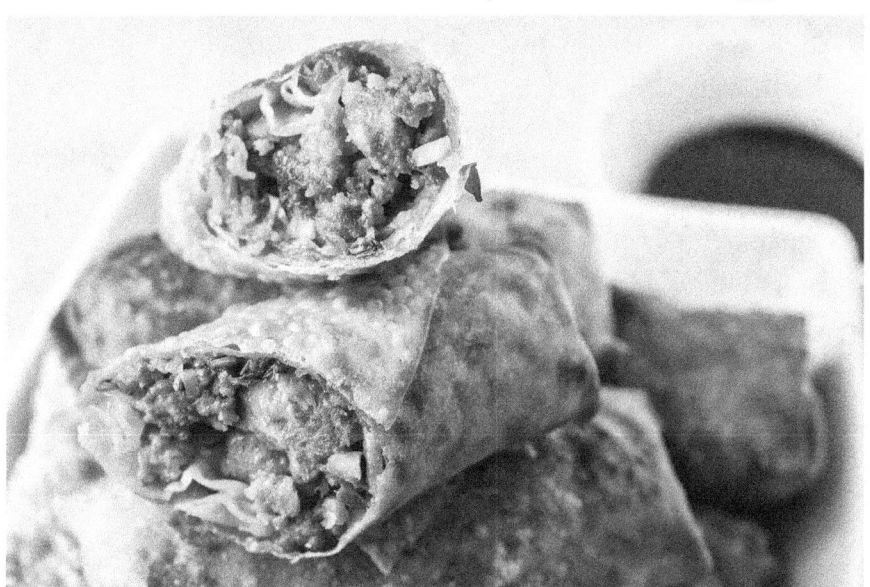

Ingredients

For the egg rolls:
- 1 Tablespoon Olive Oil
- 1 Pound Ground Pork Or Chicken
- 1 Clove Garlic, Minced
- 1 Tablespoon Grated Fresh Ginger
- 1 Medium Carrot, Shredded
- 3 Scallions, Chopped
- 3 Cups Shredded Green Cabbage
- 1 Tablespoon Soy Sauce
- 1 Tablespoon Rice Wine Vinegar

Course:
Cuisine:
Prep Time: 20 minutes
Cook Time: 25 minutes
Total Time: 18 minutes
Servings: 12 egg rolls

- 12 Egg Roll Wrappers
- Oil, For Brushing

For dipping:
- Duck sauce
- Plum sauce
- Soy sauce

Directions

1. Pour hot water over bean sprouts in a small bowl; let stand 5 minutes. Drain.
2. Meanwhile, in a Dutch oven, cook chicken over medium heat until no longer pink, 6-8 minutes, breaking into crumbles. Add green onions, ginger and garlic. Cook 1 minute longer; drain.
3. Stir in 1/2 cup Chinese-style sauce, fish sauce and soy sauce; transfer to a large bowl. Wipe pan clean.
4. In the same pan, cook and stir coleslaw mix, spinach and drained bean sprouts until crisp-tender, 4-5 min. 5. Stir into chicken mixture. Cool slightly.
6. Preheat air fryer to 400°. With one corner of an egg roll wrapper facing you, place 1/3 cup filling just below center of wrapper. (Cover remaining wrappers with a damp paper towel until ready to use.)
7. Fold bottom corner over filling; moisten remaining wrapper edges with water.
8. Fold side corners toward center over filling. Roll egg roll up tightly, pressing at tip to seal. Repeat.
9. In batches, arrange egg rolls in a single layer in greased air-fryer basket; spritz with cooking spray.
10. Cook until golden brown, 8-12 minutes. Turn; spritz with additional cooking spray.
11. Cook golden brown, 4-6 minutes longer. Serve with remaining Chinese-style sauce.

Air-Fryer Pepper Poppers

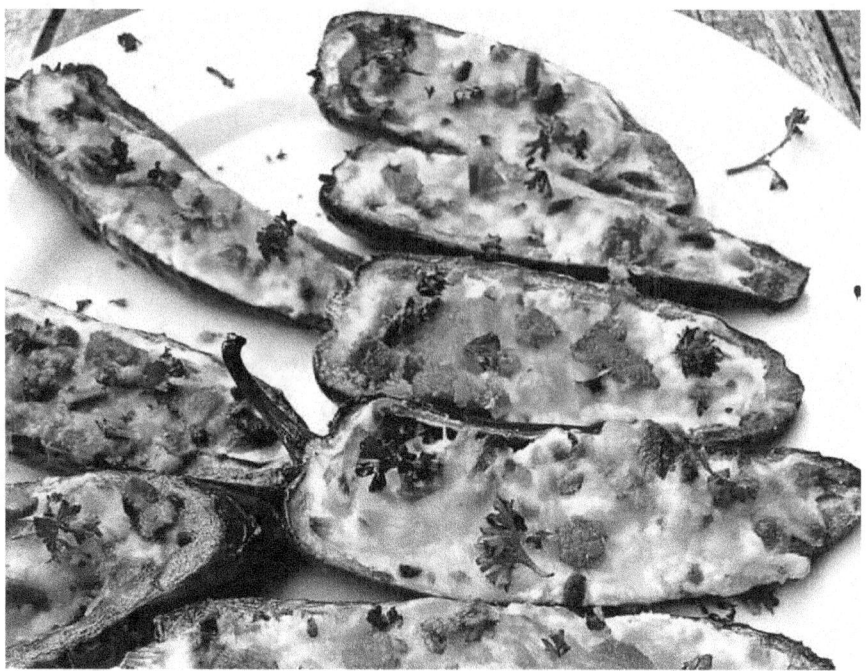

Ingredients

- 1 Package (8 Ounces) Cream Cheese, Softened
- 3/4 Cup Shredded Cheddar Cheese
- 3/4 Cup Shredded Monterey Jack Cheese
- 6 Bacon Strips, Cooked And Crumbled
- 1/4 Teaspoon Salt
- 1/4 Teaspoon Garlic Powder
- 1/4 Teaspoon Chili Powder
- 1/4 Teaspoon Smoked Paprika
- 1 Pound Fresh Jalapenos, Halved Lengthwise And Seeded
- 1/2 Cup Dry Bread Crumbs
- Optional: Sour Cream, French Onion Dip And Ranch Salad Dressing

Course:
Cuisine: American
Prep Time: 10 minutes
Cook Time:5 minutes
Total Time: 15 minutes
Servings: 5

Directions

- Preheat air fryer to 325°. In a large bowl, combine the cheeses, bacon and seasonings; mix well.
- Spoon 1-1/2 to 2 tablespoonfuls into each pepper half. Roll in bread crumbs.
- Spritz fryer basket with cooking spray.
- Working in batches if needed, place poppers in a single layer in basket.
- Cook until cheese is melted and heated through, 15-20 minutes.
- If desired, serve with sour cream, dip or dressing.

Air-Fryer Greek Breadsticks

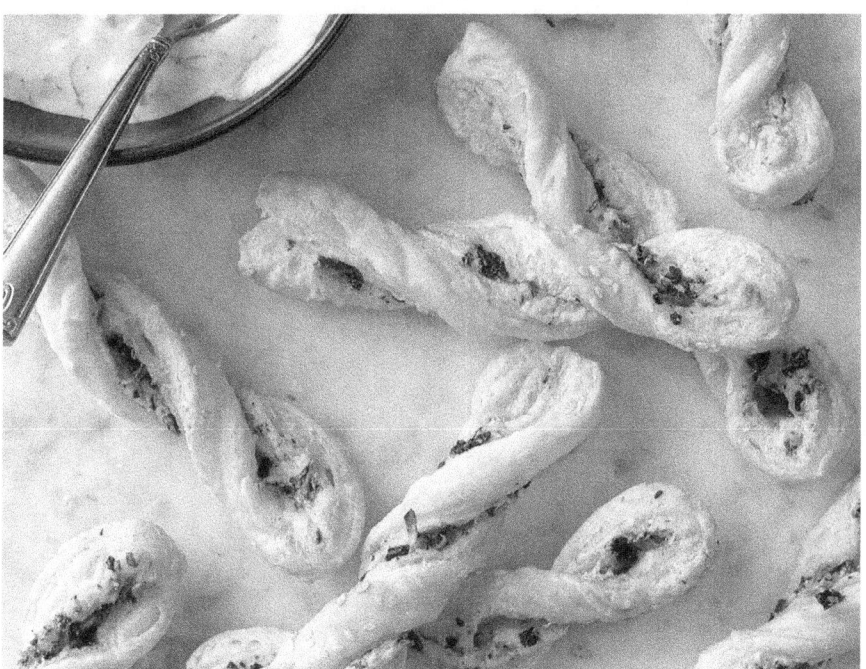

Ingredients

- 1/4 Cup Marinated Quartered Artichoke Hearts, Drained
- 2 Tablespoons Pitted Greek Olives
- 1 Package (17.3 Ounces) Frozen Puff Pastry, Thawed
- 1 Carton (6-1/2 Ounces) Spreadable Spinach
  And Artichoke Cream Cheese
- 2 Tablespoons Grated Parmesan Cheese
- 1 Large Egg
- 1 Tablespoon Water
- 2 Teaspoons Sesame Seeds

Course:
Cuisine: American
Prep Time: 20 minutes
Cook Time: 15 minutes
Total Time: 35 minutes
Servings: 32 breadsticks

Directions

• Place artichokes and olives in a food processor; cover and pulse until finely chopped. Unfold 1 pastry sheet on a lightly floured surface; spread half the cream cheese over half of pastry. Top with half the artichoke mixture. Sprinkle with half the Parmesan cheese. Fold plain half over filling; press gently to seal.
• Repeat with remaining pastry, cream cheese, artichoke mixture and Parmesan cheese. Whisk egg and water; brush over tops. Sprinkle with sesame seeds. Cut each rectangle into sixteen 3/4-in.-wide strips. Twist strips several times.
• In batches, arrange bread sticks in a single layer on greased tray in air-fryer basket. Cook until golden brown, 12-15 minutes. Serve warm with tzatziki sauce if desired.

Air Fryer Churros

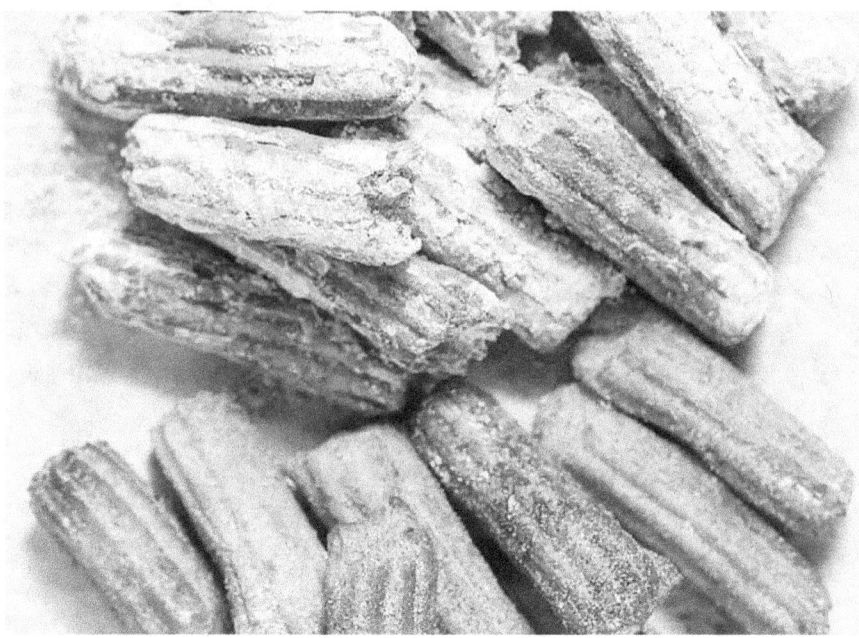

Ingredients

- Water
- Unsalted Butter
- Sugar
- Salt
- All-Purpose Flour
- Eggs
- Vanilla Extract
- Oil Spray

Course:
Cuisine: American
Prep Time: 4 minutes
Cook Time:12-15 minutes
Total Time: 18 minutes
Servings: 1 slices

Directions

Step 1. Stir together water, butter, salt, and 2 tablespoons of the sugar in a large saucepan over medium-high; cook, stirring occasionally, and bring to a boil. Turn off heat, and immediately add flour all at once and stir until well combined.

Step 2. Transfer dough to a stand mixer fitted with a paddle attachment. Beat on low speed to cool mixture slightly, about 2 minutes. Add eggs, 1 at a time, beating on medium-low until each egg is incorporated. Beat in vanilla. Increase speed to medium, and beat until mixture is cooled to room temperature, about 8 minutes.

Step 3. Chill dough 10 minutes. Place dough in piping bag fitted with a wide star tip.

Step 4. Preheat air fryer to 400°F. Spray air fryer basket with cooking spray. Pipe dough into 4-inch strips directly onto fryer basket, and cut end with kitchen shears. Lightly coat tops with cooking spray. Close lid, and cook until golden and slightly crisp, 6 to 8 minutes, flipping half way through; set aside. Repeat process with remaining dough in batches.

Step 5. Stir together cinnamon and remaining 3/4 cup sugar in a shallow dish. Brush each churro with melted butter, and dredge in cinnamon sugar. Serve immediately with chocolate sauce or dulce de leche, if desired.

Air-Fryer Baked Apples

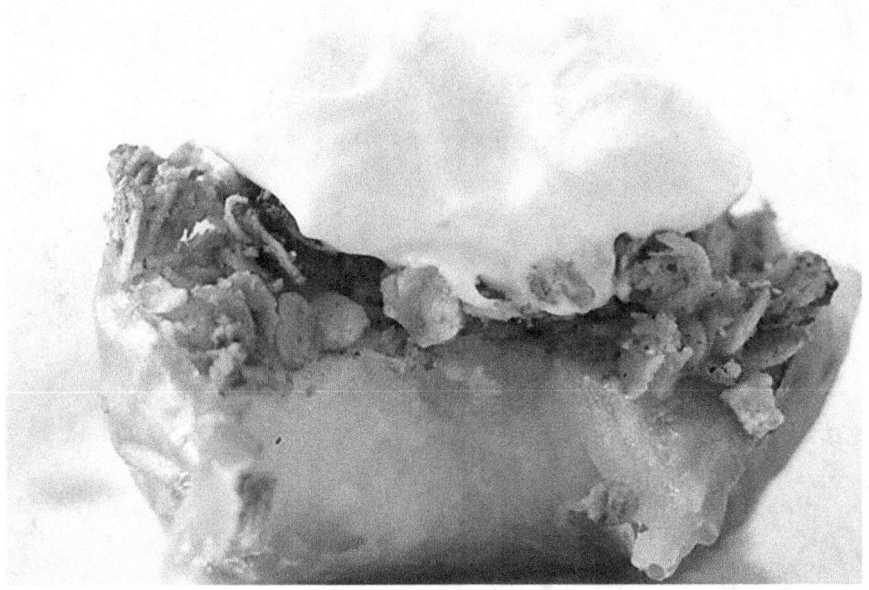

Ingredients

- 2 Apples
- 1 tsp Butter, melted
- ½ tsp Cinnamon

Topping Ingredients

- ⅓ Cup Old Fashioned / Rolled Oats
- 1 Tbsp Butter, Melted
- 1 Tbsp Maple Syrup (Or Honey Or Rice Malt Syrup)
- 1 Tsp Wholemeal / Whole Wheat Flour,
  (Can Sub For Almond Meal Or All Purpose Flour /Plain Flour)
- ½ Tsp Cinnamon

Course:
Cuisine: American
Prep Time: 4 minutes
Cook Time:12-15 minutes
Total Time: 18 minutes
Servings: 1 slices

Directions

1. Preheat the air fryer on 180C / 350F by either using the preheat setting or running your air fryer for 5 minutes on that temperature.

2. Cut apples in half through the stem and use a knife or a spoon to remove the core, stem and seeds. Brush a tsp of butter evenly over the cut sides of the apples, then sprinkle over ½ tsp of cinnamon.

3. Mix topping ingredients together in a small bowl, then spoon on top of the apple halves evenly.

4. Place the apple halves carefully into the air fryer basket, then cook for 15 minutes or until softened.

5. Serve warm with ice cream or cream if desired.

Air-Fryer English Muffin Pizzas

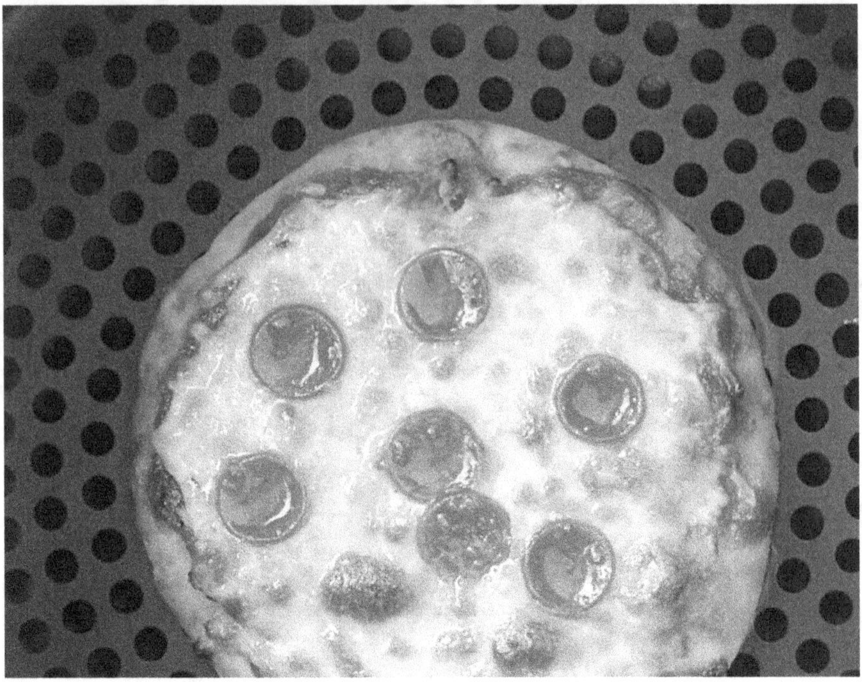

![pizza image]

Ingredients

- 1 Whole English Muffins
- 2 Teaspoons Butter (Optional)

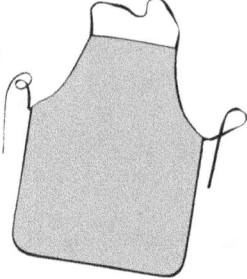

Course: Breakfast
Cuisine: American
Prep Time: 5 minutes
Cook Time: 5 minutes
Total Time: 10 minutes
Servings: 2

Directions

1. Start by putting your uncut English Muffin onto a cutting board.
2. Using a fork (remember they are fork split English Muffins, see the package for more details)
3. Place your split English Muffin into your air fryer basket.
4. Set the temperature for 400 degrees F. (Set the time for 2 minutes).
5. Remove your English Muffin, top with butter (totally optional)
6. Plate, serve and enjoy!

Keywords: how to toast an english muffin in an air fryer how to make toast in air fryer air fryer english muffin pizza toast muffin in air fryer english muffin in air fryer toast buns in air fryer chefman air fryer toast toast in nuwave air fryer

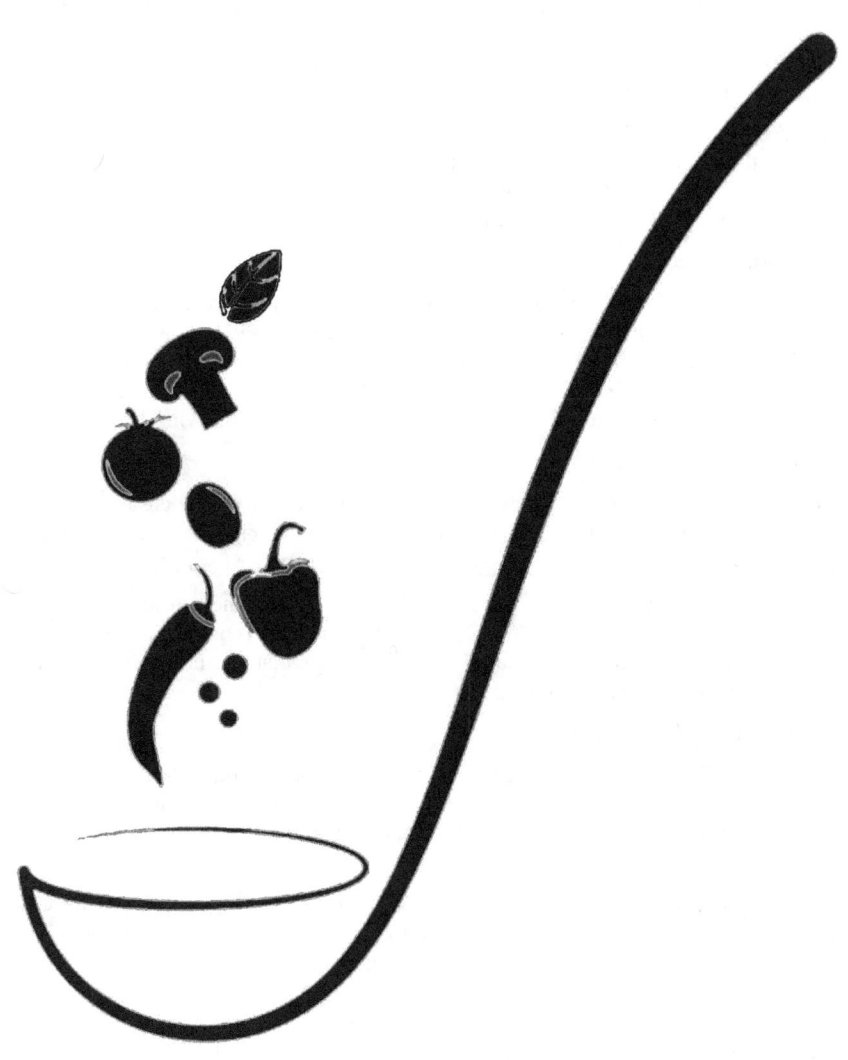

AIR FRYER VS. OVEN:
What's the Difference and Which Is Healthier?

If you have a convection oven, do you really need an air fryer to make air fryer recipes? We settle the air fryer vs. oven debate.

Not too long ago, we demystified the air fryer craze and spilled the beans about whether we thought they were worth the investment. The question keeps coming up, though: What's the difference between air frying and baking? We see it on Reddit forums and Facebook feeds, so we decided to break it down.

First, what is an air fryer?

An air fryer is a compact, countertop appliance that uses convection heating to circulate air around your food. The food is held inside in a basket and a fan rapidly moves air around the food, surrounding it in a similar way to food submerged in hot oil in a deep fryer. In the end, it works well to give food that crispy, fried texture without a lot of additional fat. Air fryers use little to no oil to get the same effect as traditional deep frying.

How is air frying different from baking in an oven?

Conventional ovens work by producing heat from an element (either gas or electric). The heat is slowly dispersed through the oven over time. In the case of convection ovens, that time is sped up by the use of a fan—similar to the one in an air fryer.

On the other hand, air fryers use rapid air technology to create heat instead of an element. That helps them heat up much more quickly than an oven (not to mention that they're much, much smaller, too). That small size helps them circulate the heat more evenly, crisping up your food without hot spots.

Which method is healthier?

Here's the real question: Is the air fryer healthier than baking food in the oven? With the air fryer, you don't need to use any oil at all. That's because the unit heats up so it's hot enough to crisp your food without any added oil. I can't say that I've ever been able to achieve that in an oven (even a convection oven).

This being said, if little to no oil is being added to the dishes you're making in the air fryer, those dishes are just as healthy as if you would have baked them. The nutritionals aren't changing, just the methodology, so air fry to your heart's content!

The bottom line

If you have the money to invest in a new appliance and the space to store it, then go for it! The air fryer gives you the crunchy texture of fried foods without the extra grease and fat. These are our Test Kitchen's favorite models.

Air-Fryer Cooking Chart

FOOD	TEMPERATURE	AIR-FRYER TIME
Bacon	400°F	5-10 minutes
Burgers	350°F	8-10 minutes
Meatballs	400°F	7-10 minutes
Steak	400°F	7-14 minutes
Pork Chops	375°F	12-15 minutes
Chicken Breast	375°F	22-23 minutes
Chicken Thighs	400°F	25 minutes
Chicken Tenders	400°F	14-16 minutes
Chicken Wings	375°F	10-12 minutes
Shrimp	375°F	8 minutes
Salmon	400°F	5-7 minutes
Cauliflower	400°F	10-12 minutes
Zucchini	400°F	12 minutes
Pickles	400°F	14-20 minutes
Potato Chips	360°F	15-17 minutes
Potato Fries	400°F	10-20 minutes
Brussels Sprouts	350°F	15-18 minutes
Pasta (Tortellini, Ravioli)	350°F	8 minutes

The tricky thing will air-fryers is that their temperatures can vary a bit. That's why we give a time range on most of these foods. When cooking seafood and meat, it doesn't hurt to check with a meat thermometer just to be on the safe side until you get to know your air fryer's temperatures down pat.

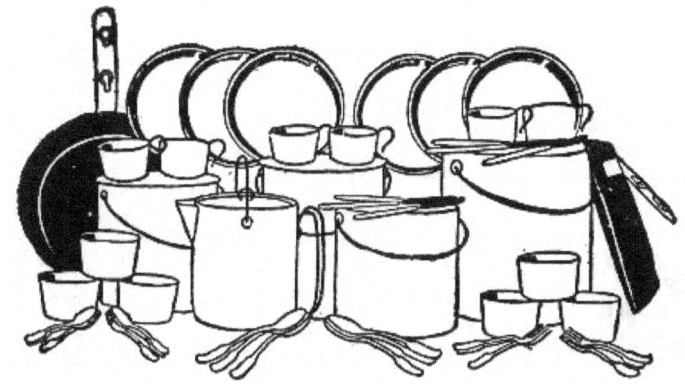

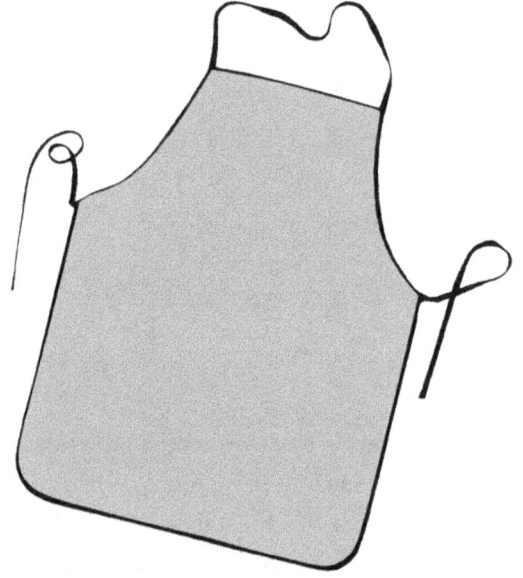